Praise for *Wacky on the Junk*

"Kathy Varner's freewheeling memoir *Wacky on the Junk* takes readers on an engaging and spirited journey fueled by sugar (and a few other substances) and told with heart. If you came of age in the era of Wonder Bread and the Grateful Dead, this book speaks your language—and if you, like Varner, feel you were airdropped on the Island of Life, *Wacky On The Junk* might just have some of the survival tools you need."

— Anne Sofee, author of *Snake Hips: Belly Dancing and How I Found True Love*

". . . an honest and candid account of a young woman's coming of age. . . . Kathy shows just how positively one can turn a seemingly hopeless life around and become a more complete person, by pure depth of character or simply growing up and seeing the error of one's ways. Thought-provoking and reflective. . . ."

—Matt McAvoy, author of *Granjy's Eyes*, *Kill the Witch!*, *Clouds*, and *The Black Line*

Wacky on the Junk

Kathy Varner

WACKY
on the
JUNK

BELLE ISLE BOOKS
www.belleislebooks.com

ISBN: 978-1-951565-13-8
LCCN: 2019917196

Cover and interior designed by Michael Hardison
Project managed by Haley Simpkiss

Printed in the United States of America

Published by
Belle Isle Books (an imprint of Brandylane Publishers, Inc.)
5 S. 1st Street
Richmond, Virginia 23219

BELLE ISLE BOOKS
www.belleislebool

belleislebooks.com | brandylanepublishers.com

I dedicate this book to my idol, author Mary Karr

To my family

And to Thomas

Introduction

When I was young and spry, I stayed up late every weeknight to watch the *Late Show with David Letterman*. I never missed an episode, but one of his skits always stuck with me: Letterman runs up to random strangers on the street and asks them a series of rapid-fire questions. "Where are you from? What do you do for a living? How are the hot dogs in Kentucky? *ARE YOU WACKY ON THE JUNK?*" The responses varied from startled blinks and stammering to confused chuckles, until he got to one guy who just shook his head as if to say, *Oh, yeah, I'm definitely wacky on the junk.*

When I initially got the idea to write this book, that phrase stuck in my mind, and the more I wrote, the better it seemed to fit. Also, I just love David Letterman. So the title stuck.

My name is Kathy. I used to pronounce it "Kaffy." Learning how to pronounce my name properly was the first order of business when I was in speech therapy. I've been to a few types of therapy in my time, some more successful than others, but I am happy to report that I can pronounce my name. I find it makes for more confident introductions.

To say I'm a sensitive and emotional soul is a study in understatement. It's like saying Joseph Stalin had "a bit of a temper." My disposition is as much a part of my genetic code as my blue eyes. Were you ever to visit the inside of my head, I'm 98 percent sure you would immediately start looking for the emergency exit—and I wouldn't blame you.

I'm fifty-three years old. I'm a paralegal, a wife, a mother of three, and a lover of music, art, nature, laughter, and food. I've spent the past nineteen years working for four attorneys who specialize in child abuse cases. Unsolicited advice: don't do that. Four attorneys is about three attorneys too many, and for someone whose opinion of the human race was already pretty low, the job has only served to verify my suspicions. Perhaps I'd have a better outlook if I took up flower delivery.

⁓

I live in Richmond, Virginia—a historic city with great restaurants and breweries, a beautiful river, an amazing art museum, great live music, and a top-notch annual folk festival. Richmond, locally known as RVA, rocks—but for God's sake, don't tell anyone. We don't want everyone and their brother moving here.

What follows herein are stories—some poignant, some of the sorts of things everyone goes through, all told through the voice of someone who often feels like a foreigner air-dropped onto the Island of Life—with no survival tools.

-1-

I'm fairly confident I was the result of one of my parents'
many cocktail parties—conceived after much imbib-
ing of Manhattans and martinis. Mom was thirty-six years
old at the time, and my father forty-three, with four kids
already, ages twelve, ten, eight, and five.

My parents are not Mike and Carol Brady. I imagine
Mom announcing my impending birth to my father. His
response: "Oh, for crying out loud!"

ɛↄ

At age five, I love my parents' cocktail parties. I get to don
my favorite purple velvet dress with fancy gold embroidery.
Mom strategically places me in the hallway, away from the
foyer where the guests arrive, but close enough for me to
catch a glimpse of their dashing outfits.

Dad's colleagues from the college where he teaches and my
parents' friends from the church choir arrive at our home.
They greet me with a cordial rub on my head, or hand me a
coat to hang up.

Sitting down is not my strong suit, but I take a seat in the
living room, excited to be in the room that is off-limits at
any other time. The room comes alive with puffs of smoke,
plaid suits, fancy dresses, salutes with delicate cone-shaped
drinking glasses, dishes filled with mixed nuts and mints,
laughter, and discussions of matters I pretend to understand.

As the party progresses, the guests get friendlier. Mr. McGruder pulls me over to his chair and tells me to sit on his lap. When he starts bouncing me on his leg, I think it's unoriginal. Mr. McGruder's shirt smells odd, and he's holding a drink that has a green olive floating on top. He is clearly a weird man. I wiggle away.

Then comes the dreaded announcement from Mom: "Bedtime." I lie in my bed upstairs, the taste of mints still fresh in my mouth. Mom sings to me every night before bed, but not tonight. I'm restless.

The sounds of widespread amusement and heels clicking against the wood floors grow in volume and boisterousness as the party gets into full swing. I long to get a closer look, to see what the adults do when no children are present.

I move to the top of the stairwell and perch there with my thumb in my mouth, tucking my long cotton nightgown under my knees and my frayed blanket into the crook of my elbow. I used to slide down this stairwell for fun. *Bumpity, bump, bump, bump* down the steps, then back up and *bumpity, bump, bump, bump* back down. The fact that I park myself at the top like an obedient child is quite impressive in retrospect. I watch as guests pass from the living room to the den. I decide that when I grow up, I want to be svelte and wear cat-eye glasses and a smart updo, and smoke cigarettes like the women downstairs. I'll sip a drink with a cherry on top, not the drink with the olive.

Shouldn't the bumpity-bump situation have been a clue for my parents to call the Early Intervention hotline? "Yes, hi," Mom would say. "Should I be concerned that my child is sliding down the stairs on her butt around five hundred times consecutively? Why, yes, she was a difficult birth. What has she eaten today? Frosted Wheaties; Pop-Tarts; and two, or maybe five, glasses of Tang. Why do you ask?"

❧

Mom and I spend a lot of time together while my father works at the college as a band director. I lie in front of the TV, anxious for my all-time favorite scene to appear—the downpour of ping-pong balls on Captain Kangaroo's head. I love it so much, I celebrate by running through the kitchen, down the hall, and through the den—around, around, and around in an enthusiastic display of my love for Mr. Moose.

Mom sits at the Formica table in the kitchen, smoking a cigarette, drinking coffee, and lost in a book. She is a comforting presence, with her bright blue eyes and pretty face. She is patient to a fault—and likely in denial that a roadrunner on ten shots of espresso lives in her house.

❧

Whenever Mom goes out to direct the women's chorus or to practice with the choral guild, Iris comes to look after me and clean the house.

I dread her arrival. It's Iris and me and a whole lot of boring. Iris doesn't allow me to slide down the stairwell or run wild around the house. Today, I decide I've had enough of Iris.

After Iris arrives, I escape out the front door and chase after Mom. She is inching the Chevy Impala down the street like an anxious driver who did not get her license until she was well into her thirties—which, of course, she is. She drives so slowly that my stubby little legs catch up to her within a few blocks. I plead through the window for her to come back home. She smiles and waves, and then Iris snatches me up.

Iris is so mad. "Don't you ever run away like that again, you hear?"

After that little escapade, Iris makes me watch her clean the house. I sit on the couch while Iris vacuums, and pick up a copy of *Life* magazine from the coffee table. I open it to a photo of a woman raising her arms in the air. She looks like she is losing her mind. I relate to that woman. I don't know it at the time, but this photo is my first introduction to the Woodstock music festival.

The pervasive scent of Pledge is a cruel reminder of my boring existence. I flip through the photos in the magazine. I'm six years old, and I don't know what to make of them. *That's a whole, whole, whole bunch of people—oh, look, it's a clown. It must be a party. There's a school bus and kids—that's a much more colorful school bus than I've ever seen. It's a big party—in the mud—and one of the teachers is taking a nap on a motorcycle.*

I laugh at the strange spectacle. I want an invitation to the party.

When Mom returns home, I make a beeline out the front door and run down the street to find a neighborhood friend to play with me. Nobody is around, so I go to Ms. McCartney's house to talk to the old man who works odd jobs for her.

The old man is hauling a lawn mower bag to the woods to dump it out. He's a big man—around three hundred pounds. He looks distracted by body aches and the weight of life. He takes a seat on a five-gallon bucket next to the grey concrete lawn ornament that possesses the magical ability to reveal the time of day by its shadow.

The man takes a long drink from his thermos and picks up a flat, greyish shell from a pile next to the bucket. He wipes away more sweat, then he tips a slimy globule from the shell into his mouth.

"*Ewww!* What is that?" I've never seen an oyster before.

The old man offers me one from the pile. I jump back in fear of the oyster and run home.

My father and my brother Robert are watching TV in the den while Mom cooks supper. I'm out of breath. "The man working at Ms. McCartney's house is so poor, he fetches his meals from the creek!"

Robert laughs. Dad isn't paying attention.

Robert is my parents' only son, and five years my senior. He had a medical emergency when he was fifteen months old. The local hospital couldn't help him, so he was flown in a helicopter to the best hospital in the state. Mom told me he stopped breathing for about three minutes. I bet it was the worst three minutes of my parents' lives.

The ordeal caused Robert some brain damage. He attends school and functions well in my mind, but he suffers horrible allergies. For a long time, I thought his chronic stuffy nose was the cause of his issues.

I take a seat on the couch next to Robert. He is still laughing over my creek comment. He's the Keeper of the Dorito Bag. I beg him over and over for the bag. He gives me one Dorito, laughs, and says, "You only get one, stupid." Then he holds the bag up high, out of my reach.

Robert's shenanigans are a constant feature in my life. I ignore him most of the time, but sometimes he sits on my face and rips out a stinky blow from his butt. That gets a rise out of me.

Mom announces, "Dinner's ready."

It's Hamburger Helper Night, with butterscotch pudding for dessert. After finishing a second helping of pudding, I rock back and forth, swinging my legs like a spastic metronome, waiting for my cue. Mom finally says, "You can go outside and play now, honey."

I'm up at "You can" and out the front door before she's done talking. I hear kids yelling, "The Smoker Man is coming!" I run down the street and join the gathering of neighborhood kids.

The Smoker Man's truck approaches with a whirring sound. We stand on the curb and wave as it passes by. Then we jump and dance around in the cloud of dichlorodiphenyltrichloroethane—otherwise known as the mosquito-killer DDT—that it leaves in its wake.

Years later, while introducing myself to a new therapist, I tell her I'm not sure what exactly caused my issues—but I'm willing to bet it was either the diet of Frosted Wheaties, Tang, and Pop Tarts; the gallons of antibiotics I took for my many ear infections; the endocrine-disrupting effects of the DDT; or some toxic combination thereof. Also, my mother often implied that I may have been brain-damaged at birth. And then, of course, there was that one time I tried riding my bicycle down Ms. Deboard's concrete steps, just to see what would happen. You can guess the answer: a concussion, and a trip to the emergency room.

∾

Mom and I often picnic at the lake, which lies a short walk through the woods from our house.

The lake is owned by the college where my father works. All around it, short trails branch from the main path and travel down to the water's edge. I run down every one of them, tapping my foot on top of the water and inspecting the area for fish and turtles.

Birdsong and rummaging squirrels command my attention. I gaze at the still lake. The sound of the gently rippling water comforts me. The lake is a serenade for my soul.

Sometimes I can hear a college football game in the distance. My father is with us, directing the brass, woodwinds, and percussion in a festive march muted by the buildings and trees. It's a peppy backdrop to the comfortable silence between Mom and me.

Every time we embark on a picnic, we follow the exact same routine: we walk the path along the lake. I run up a short hill to the rim of a large hollow about twenty-five feet wide by twenty feet deep. I always thought it was a Revolutionary War trench, but I don't know for sure.

I run down to the bottom and back up until I'm exhausted. Mom waits patiently at the top. When I'm done, she takes my dirty hand, and we continue down the path to a wooden bridge that crosses a stream. I run ahead of Mom to the bridge to look for crayfish and salamanders. Then, when she reaches me, we turn around and walk to a smooth, earthy clearing above the lake for our picnic.

Mom pulls out the same lunch she makes me throughout my entire childhood: a slice of a square flimsy orange thing posing as cheese on Wonder bread, a Little Debbie Oatmeal Crème Pie or a Twinkie, an apple, and Welch's grape juice. I would have lost my mind if I ever bit into a PB&J sandwich or tried a sip of cranberry juice.

❧

Breakfast is either Fruit Loops, Frosted Wheaties, or some other cereal that contains a huge amount of sugar. I get it. I cannot imagine raising five kids. My hat is off to Mom for managing to feed us instead of just locking herself in a closet and screaming.

Still, starting my day off with Frosted Wheaties is a bad plan. I crash midmorning. I sit in class at school and stare out the window, watching kids on the playground and squirrels gathering acorns. Meanwhile, the teacher gives a lecture on vowel sounds.

My nose is stuffy and my head feels like it's filled with pudding. My social skills are awkward at best. I have so many ear infections that the chalky pink medicine I'm forced to take could almost be a food group.

My second-grade math teacher, Ms. Devigne, has it out for me. Looking back, I think she was in the throes of menopause. At least, I hope she was—otherwise, her life was one giant bad mood, with a side helping of mean. She often calls on me to answer questions.

"Kathy, if John pays four dollars for eight apples, how much would he pay for twelve apples?"

"I don't know, Ms. Devigne."

"Class, once again Kathy doesn't know the answer." She walks over to my desk. Her face is as white as her chalky hands. She turns to my desk neighbor. "I bet Sue here knows the answer."

She does, and after giving it, Sue turns my way and shoots me a look that is so snotty, it becomes my visual reference point for the word "snotty" for the rest of my life. My face turns redder than a Japanese maple in autumn.

I think Sue Meyer won the genetic lottery. Straight-A student with tons of friends and beautiful long, thick red hair. However, she lost out on the kindness factor and I, being her desk neighbor, am frequently the recipient of comments like, "Hey, Kathy, who dressed you up in that stupid outfit? Tell your mother to get her glasses checked." I want to go home, but instead I go to speech therapy after class to learn how to pronounce my *R*s.

∽

Summer break comes not a moment too soon. We pack up the Chevy Impala for the annual two-week vacation at the Outer Banks in North Carolina. Packing a car for a two-week vacation for a family of seven requires a scientific approach, but my father has mastered it.

Dad spends the entire morning arranging boxes and suitcases in the trunk and on the roof rack. It's a solo gig. God forbid anyone in the family place something in the trunk: "What in tarnation are you doing? That's not where it goes!"

Dad is drenched in sweat. He carefully lays his fishing rods on top of the packed trunk and shuts the lid. "Is the house locked up? Windows down? Okay, let's hit the road!" The seven of us pile into the car.

At home, I don't see much of my sisters. They are off at

college, working, or otherwise avoiding the roadrunner in the house. But now, we are making up for lost time. Whether they like it or not, their seven-year-old sister is sandwiched next to them in the back seat, and I am not shutting up. "Do you like college? What's it like? What do candy stripers do? Do you get to eat candy? Do you have any candy? Do you have a boyfriend? What are you reading? What's it about? Are we almost there?"

Dad drives along the interstate with his arm hanging out the window. Everyone prays my sister Kris doesn't get carsick. Dad hollers, "If it wasn't for all you stinking kids, I'd be driving that shiny new Cadillac to my second home in Florida." Everyone laughs. I continue my onslaught of questions until my father has had enough. "For crying out loud, shut your trap." I do. Then I knock my knees together, as frantic as my nonstop chattering.

We arrive at the old white clapboard bungalow and bolt out of the car—the family to the sanity of personal space, and I to greet the glorious ocean, the sand dunes, the tall reeds. Then a run under the house, a peek into the old outdoor shower, and a final lap through the cottage and out to the wraparound porch, inhaling the salty air, rejoicing that I'm back in paradise.

ॐ

I take a seat on the porch swing. A seat on the swing is difficult to get, but the back-and-forth squeal is as much a part of the beach experience as the crashing waves.

Dad is down on the beach, fishing. He's in his element, wearing his usual beach attire: a white canvas bucket hat that stands up on his head, accentuating his goofy personality; cream swim trunks; and white socks, so that the tops of his feet don't burn. He's handsome, like Humphrey Bogart, and unassuming, except for the fact that he is wearing socks on the beach. He stands next to his fishing pole, which is propped in its holder, the line cast into the ocean. Every so often, he reaches over to the pole and reels the line in a bit. He's as smooth at fishing as he is at playing swing jazz on his saxophone.

Then he catches sight of a school of bluefish. He grabs the pole and takes off running down the beach to try to snag one, in all his white-socked glory—no longer a smooth fisherman.

I run down to the shoreline to see if there are any fish in the bucket. Robert sits in the sand, poking the eyeballs out of a fish head. I find the scene disgusting.

I point to the ocean and say, "Why can't the fish stay in their home instead of having their eyeballs poked out by a creep like you?" Robert laughs and pretends to flick an eyeball at me.

Robert and I wait for our sisters to come to the beach. We are not allowed to swim unattended. Still, this is the first year Dad doesn't require twelve-year-old Robert to wear a life jacket—a restriction I think is set about six years later than necessary. I don a bright orange life jacket and bob up and down in the ocean. Sometimes a wave gives me a swift push. My siblings are swimming and riding the waves, free as the seagulls that fly above us. It's a thrill I cannot wait to experience.

Dad comes running to the shore. "Get out now. There's a

storm coming." He waves his arm toward the cottage, then runs behind us like he's herding cows. The thunder sounds like it's a hundred miles away, but Dad is prepared for a miracle bolt of lightning to take out the lot of us.

We change out of our wet bathing suits and gather on the porch to watch the storm. Dad leads the laughter. The jokes go over my head, but I laugh anyway, charmed by his wit.

Sheets of rain blow onto the porch and break up the party. Dad and the three oldest gather inside for a game of pinochle. Mom is on the other side of the wall, singing an opera while she cooks supper. I stay on the porch swing with Robert, our legs swinging in harmony as we laugh and catch the raindrops with our feet, waiting for the sky to clear so we can play on the beach.

After the storm, Robert and I run to the shoreline. Baby sand crabs burrow frantically into the smooth wet sand, before a wave covers the scene with white foam. I find a conch shell and hold it to my ear. "I can hear the ocean. Bet you can't."

Robert says, "That's because the ocean is right here, dummy. I'll race you to the house."

We run back up to the porch swing. I watch a ship sail along the horizon. It's a thousand miles away, in the land where the sun is born.

After supper, the family gathers at the shore. Dad, Robert, and my oldest sister, Cindy, place bloodworms on their fishhooks. I look away in disgust. Mom takes my hand, and we stroll along the beach, gathering shells. I find a creamy white shell embellished with dark purple and lavender. A miracle from the sea.

Robert gives up on catching fish and joins us. Sand crabs scramble across our path. I'm terrified. Robert hoists me onto his back and gives me a ride to the cottage.

Mom puts me to bed at eight o'clock on the dot. My Dad and sisters are on the other side of the bedroom wall, playing a lively game of pinochle. Evening light shines through the shade that covers the window. It beckons me to escape, to get away from the dark clapboard walls that surround me.

I go to the bathroom even though I don't need to, and stop by the game to take a peek. The entire pinochle crew says, "Get back to bed!"

I do, and after what seems like an eternity, the crashing waves and the wind that knocks the wooden shutters finally rock me to sleep.

The two weeks at the beach fly by. When we get back home, the forest behind our house is a dense contrast to the open sky and ocean. The buzzing sounds of cicadas are a countdown to the dreaded beginning of school, just a few weeks away.

-2-

Travis Miller and I have known each other since first grade. Our effortless relationship as class and band-mates takes a turn in seventh grade band class. He's the first-chair trumpeter. From my seat in the flute section I have a direct line of sight to his gorgeous smile, and his eyes that resemble sunlit honey. I sneak a peek while he's talking to Steve Connor, the second chair. The way Travis crosses his leg and holds his trumpet makes for a perfect pairing of corduroy and brass.

If Travis Miller were ever to learn of my affections, I would run away and hide in the instrument closet. I'm sixteen pounds overweight, and I still watch *Little House on the Prairie.* I am not equipped to handle Travis' inevitable rejection.

Every day after band practice, my best friend Jan and I walk to class together, past the hallway hecklers who stand against the lockers, bellowing *"Pee-yew!"* as Randy Newsome hurries by, his shaggy head hanging over his worn plaid shirt, which is so small, only two buttons remain.

After school, I sit at the kitchen table while Mom washes dishes. She has just finished teaching her last piano student of the day.

"Mom, did kids tease each other when you were my age?"

"If they did, I don't remember it. We were more worried about a Japanese invasion. Why do you ask?"

I tell Mom about the hallway bullies. "It happens all the time. I think Randy Newsome's parents are so poor, they can't buy him new clothes or wash the ones he has. How would those kids feel if they couldn't buy a new shirt?"

"Speaking of new clothes, we need to go shopping for a blouse for you. I signed you up to play in a flute recital at a church this Sunday afternoon. Make sure you practice, okay?"

"Does it require that I stand up and perform in front of people?"

"Oh, it'll be fine."

My brother could have come into the kitchen and given me a swift kick in the shins, and I would have preferred it over performing a recital in front of a crowd. I have six days to obsess over the flute solo.

❧

Mom and I arrive at the church. We take a seat in the front row. I want to run to the narthex and hide. I could fake a stomach bug. Hell, with the way my stomach feels, I'd hardly need to fake anything.

The first performance is a gospel group. The whole congregation gets on their feet, dances, and praises God to the funky beat. This church is different from the Methodist church my family attends. It's livelier.

The congregation at our Methodist church do not dance in the aisles. Then again, it's not as though "Amazing Grace" or "Holy, Holy, Holy" inspire a sudden urge to jump up, spin around, throw my arms in the air, and dance like nobody's watching. Believe me, the congregation at my church would definitely be watching.

Next up is the church choir. Their energetic hymns are much better than our Methodist choir hymns. Once again, the crowd get to their feet in a praise party of giant proportions, clapping and dancing in the aisle. I'm lost in how cool this church and their music are. Then it hits me: *Shit, I have to follow that. What kind of cruel joke is this?*

I walk over to my music stand to play a minuet in G minor, but actually it's a minuet in Major Meltdown. I can hardly get a sound out of my flute. I can hear people snickering, and I'm completely humiliated.

In retrospect, it's funny. It reminds me of the time I went to my daughter's first performance with her school orchestra. They started playing, and it was horrible. It sounded like a symphony warming up before the show, but worse. So what did I do? I busted out laughing. Nice, right?

After the recital, Mom drops me off at a Young Life meeting at our church. It's a gathering where kids get together to play games and perform skits.

Young Life is the one activity at our church that I enjoy, other than watching Gus, a man from the local hospital for the mentally ill who attends our church every so often. During the service, he stands next to the beautiful organist at the front of the sanctuary. When it's time to sing a hymn, Gus holds the hymn book high above his head and belts so loudly that the congregation sound like quiet back-up singers. Gus sings "How Great Thou Art" like Liberace on a shot of exuberance. Gus is the epitome of the hymn's title.

The Young Life meeting after the flute recital is a pizza party. I groan inwardly when I see Kathleen is there. Kathleen is another young-lifer, and all I really know about her is that she does not like me. I'm not sure why.

I'm eating a flimsy piece of pizza. Gravity is not on my side. I devour the entire slice in one big gulp, so that I don't embarrass myself by spilling the runny contents all over the place.

Kathleen picks up a slice of pizza, walks over to me, and slaps it on my new blouse. She rubs it around for good measure.

If there is a memo about how to respond to someone who invades one's space with a weapon of mass pizza destruction, I have missed it. I freeze in shock, then make a quick escape to the church parlor and wait for Mom to pick me up.

At home, I lie in my bed, sad for the effort Mom made to take me shopping for a blouse. Sad for Randy Newsome. I cannot quite bring myself to feel sad for Kathleen—or for whatever tragic backstory that may have caused her to do such a thing. All I feel is contempt for her—and for my failure to withstand that side of humanity.

∾

Every day after school, I come home and head straight to the kitchen to snack on cinnamon toast and ice cream. It's much tastier than discouragement and failure.

I grow to a size twelve, and my ballet teacher reminds me of it at every class. When I attempt to do the splits, I stop several inches from the floor. Ms. Petrov walks over, places both hands on my shoulders, and gives me a swift push. I yell out in pain.

"You too beeg to do de spleets!"

She screams it over and over, at which point I run home in tears and stuff my face with peanut butter toast covered in globs of honey just to spite Ms. Petrov. I run out the back door and toss my leotard into the tin can.

Mom is in the kitchen cooking supper. She can tell I'm upset.

"What's the matter, honey?"

I tell Mom the story, then declare, "Ms. Petrov is so mean. I want to quit ballet."

"Oh, my goodness. That wasn't very nice of her." Mom sips from her glass of wine and stirs the pot on the stove. "Oh, it's my favorite Schubert concerto." She turns up the volume on the old radio that does not do Schubert or the Saturday afternoon Metropolitan Opera any justice.

I walk into the den, sobbing. Dad looks away from Walter Cronkite and rolls his eyes.

Later that night, Dad and I are watching TV together, like we do most nights. Mom is in bed, reading one of the library books from the high stack that sits on her nightstand.

Dad calls me over to his recliner during a commercial break. I kneel on the floor next to him. He gives me a quick neck squeeze and a nudge. That's his way of saying he cares. Then he snaps his fingers and points to his neck. It's my cue to give him a neck rub.

Dad is the only person in my life who can snap his fingers at me. I know he's playing.

When I rub Dad's neck, he tells me stories. The stories are gold to me.

"I was supposed to be on the USS *Arizona,* but I injured my finger playing baseball with the fellas. I couldn't play my horn, so they kept me home until it healed. At the time I was disappointed, but then the ship was bombed during Pearl Harbor. All of my band buddies died. I've got an envelope of letters from those fellas. Got it after they all died. Do you know about Pearl Harbor, kid?"

"That was during World War II, wasn't it?" I'm proud.

"I went to college in Chicago on the GI Bill. I earned money playing jazz in the nightclubs. Back in the forties, all of the nightclubs were mob-run. One time a new fella in the band jumped up when he saw a fella in the audience slap his girl. He slapped her so hard she cried. I pulled him back down and said, 'You don't mess with these guys unless you want to end up floating in Lake Michigan.'"

Now that ballet is a bust, I embark on a baking frenzy. My sisters will be home soon for Christmas, and I cannot wait.

I pull out *The Joy of Cooking* and bake wedding cookies, lemon squares, chocolate chips, and iced sugar cookies. There is only one problem: the Joy of Cooking turns into the Joy of Eating. Then my parents and brother follow my lead.

On Christmas morning, the whole clan gathers in the living room. Mom reads aloud the Christmas card we've received from her parents: "Merry Christmas, All. Thank you so much for the delicious salad toppings. We received them three days ago and they're almost gone."

My sister Sara cannot believe it. "You gave them salad toppings for Christmas? What the heck?"

Mom realizes what happened. "Goodness, they thought the potpourri we sent them were salad toppings!" Everyone busts out laughing. Mom looks worried.

I summon Robert to help me get the gifts for my sisters. We return and place them on the coffee table. I grin from ear to ear. "I made each of you a cheesecake. The fancy kind, in a springform pan. It comes with a jar of praline topping."

The family yells in harmony: "Wow, that's a lot of cheesecake!"

Sugar gives my foggy brain a boost. I've consumed it regularly all my life: as penny candy, Oreos, ice cream, half a cheesecake with praline topping.

I spend a lot of time in my bedroom, listening to "Dancing Queen" by Abba and dreaming of the day when I will be thin, not so awkward, and worthy of a boy like Travis Miller. I used to practice my flute every day, but now I practice eating multiple Oreos in one sitting.

෨

When I'm in my sophomore year of high school, the marching band travels to a competition in Winchester, Virginia. I board the bus and sit one row behind Travis Miller. I have a direct view of his beautiful face. Conversation is not required.

After the competition, a group of friends and I get together at our hotel. Someone pulls out a joint. I'm curious, so I take a hit. I wait for some unknown effect to hit me. Nothing happens.

I don't know where the adults are. Maybe they are off getting high, too, so they can cope with all the teenagers.

My best friend Jan is up when I enter our hotel room. "I can't believe you smoked pot. You're going to end up a loser pothead like my brother. Your life is ruined."

The weekend after the competition, my neighbor Shanti comes home from boarding school. Shanti's father is a law professor with long grey hair. Her mother is a Montessori schoolteacher. They are sweeter than a caramel apple pie. Shanti and I are the same age, but Shanti is way more advanced in the practice of naughty behavior, like doing drugs—and older men. Before my underwhelming experience on the band trip, I used to swear I would never partake in marijuana or hang out with the likes of Shanti.

A few weeks later, I'm making friendly small talk with Shanti's parents in the street in front of their house.

"Is Shanti home?"

"Yes. You can go in the house and say hello if you want."

I knock on Shanti's bedroom door. Until now, the extent of our interaction has been exchanges of polite neighborly hellos, but that's all. She is surprised to see me.

"Hey, Shanti. Guess what? I smoked pot on a band trip."

Shanti gasps. She eyes me up and down—from my Top-Siders to my Dockers, up to my pink button-down shirt with a three-bead gold necklace hung through the collar.

"Oh my God. *You* smoked pot?" She laughs.

"Yeah, but I didn't get high."

Shanti says, "I guarantee you this weed I have will get you high. It's called Space Weed."

Shanti pulls out a bong. We each take a hit. I think it's a

bit ballsy to do bong hits in her parents' house, but maybe they have some sort of an agreement. Her parents seem like hippies. Maybe getting high is a family affair. I take a hit of the Space Weed.

"Jumpin' Jack Flash" is playing. "Shanti, something is wrong with your turntable. This song is slowwwwww. 'Jumpin' Jack Flash' should be faaaaast." I stare at the turntable.

Shanti laughs. "You're super stoned." She walks over to the bedroom window and takes a hit. I wonder why the trees at Shanti's house are so much greener than the trees at my house.

Shanti's father is standing outside the window in plain view, leaning on a rake. Shanti is so high she doesn't see him—that is, not until he's seen her. Shanti turns around and says, "Oh, shit. My father just watched me take a bong hit."

Shanti's father storms into the bedroom, madder than hell. "Give me the bong."

Shanti says, "No. I paid fifty bucks for this bong. You can't have it."

I duck out while Shanti and her father duke it out. I go home and run up to my bedroom. I put on Foreigner's "Double Vision" and decide it's a disgrace to music. Besides, I'm so stoned, my own double vision is all I can handle.

I find a local pot connection. He tells me he has some speed if I want to try it. Says it will help me lose weight and study. The pills are called Yellow Jackets.

With the help of the Yellow Jackets, the fog in my brain clears, my grades improve, my bedroom is clean, and I lose weight. I read all the way through James Michener's lengthy book *Chesapeake*. It's a win-win-win-win situation.

I used to imagine a commercial, like the Nuprin commercial from the 1980s: *Little, yellow, different. When you need to focus and get stuff done. Yellow Jackets.* They're the Ritalin of my youth, if Ritalin was about fifty times more potent.

I never imagined I could be an artist, but my artistic skills blossom. A little pot and speed, and I'm drawing quality pencil sketches like nobody's business.

However, speed is not the answer to my issues. I'm pretty sure it's bad for you, and may cause heart issues, high blood pressure, and rotting teeth. I'm no expert, but I'm confident that long-term use is not the best plan.

My friends manage a healthy mix of socializing and academics during high school. I opt for the former. Academics can wait in line and pick a number—as long as it isn't $6(3x - 2) - (x - 3)$.

I'm a junior in high school. I work as a sales clerk at Peebles Department Store on weeknights and weekends. Shanti and I hang out on the weekends when she comes home from boarding school. One day, she comes into the store and says, "You need to come with me. I have some purple microdot acid. Tell them you're sick."

We get into Shanti's VW Bug. I say, "Shanti, I'm scared straight about doing acid. There's a movie about someone who's on acid and thinks he can fly. He jumps off a roof and dies."

Shanti says, "It's not like that. It makes you super happy, and you laugh a lot. C'mon, give it a try."

"Okay."

Shanti wants to visit her friend who works at the ice cream shop. The acid hits me while we're in the shop. It makes the people who are licking their ice cream cones look so weird.

I start laughing uncontrollably. Shanti starts laughing, too. She asks me what's so funny. I say, "These people eating ice cream cones." I wave my arm around the shop. The customers look at me like I've lost my mind. They're partially right.

Shanti and I take a drive along the Colonial Parkway. We park and stare into the woods. I see a lake and ducks. Then I realize there is no lake, nor ducks.

Another car pulls into the pull-off. Shanti says, "Let's go."

I say, "Yeah, let's get out of here."

We drive along the parkway. I say, "How come we had to go?"

Shanti says, "I don't know."

There's a pause. Then we bust out laughing.

We go to the bowling alley where Shanti's boyfriend works. He's fifty-something years old. Shanti is sixteen.

When we leave the bowling alley, Shanti's VW Bug is turned upside down. At first, I think I must be super high—but as it turns out, the car really is upside down. A couple of the guys who work at the bowling alley did it.

I'm laughing so hard I'm crying. Shanti is shouting at the guys. "Why would you turn my car upside down?!"

The guys are laughing. Shanti says, "IT'S NOT FUNNY!" Then she starts laughing, too.

❧

I spend a lot of days hanging out at my friend Vicky's

after school. I met Vicky in an art class. She is so talented, I imagine she was probably creating pieces worthy of Henri Matisse when she was five years old.

Vicky and her sweet brother inhabit an apartment next door to their mother and her roommate, a concept I find quite bohemian. I'm always welcome to visit. Vicky gives me art lessons, and there's a constant flow of beer. I spend a lot of time there.

Vicky's mother Julie and her roommate Jackie are artists, and friendly lushes. They love my visits. I'm a good listener to their nonstop stories, which leave me in stitches more often than not.

During one of my visits, Jackie invites me to go see her son's rock band, Bruce Olsen and the Offenders. They are playing at William and Mary Hall, which is a big deal for them.

Julie finishes her glass of whiskey and sets it down with the force of the epiphany she just had. "Why don't you invite your mother to join us? It'll be a blast." We all laugh—Julie and Jackie in inebriated joy, and I at the concept of my Mom joining us at a rock concert.

Mom agrees to go without knowing anything about the band. She dons her Mostly Mozart Festival T-shirt, comfy blue cotton pants, and Hush Puppies. It's the hippest outfit she owns.

The concert hall is filled to maybe five percent of capacity. The rest of the hall serves as an echo board for the loud, hard-driving rock band. The volume is painful.

Julie and Jackie dance for the entire show, swinging their arms in the air, hootin' and hollerin', and nipping from a flask between songs. Mom sits next to me with her head down and her hands over her ears. She looks like she wishes she had remembered her book and earplugs. I worry Mom will suffer hearing loss. Her piano students will never forgive me.

The day after the concert, I walk into the kitchen at home. "Hi, Mom. Now you can say you've experienced a rock concert."

Mom says, "What? My ears are still ringing."

℮℈

My parents have no clue how to deal with my shenanigans. They are freaked out, so they send me to a psychologist. I'm told to look at inkblots and describe what I see.

I say, "It looks like two cliffs on the edge of a body of water. Each cliff has a polar bear hanging from it. Also, I'm very stoned right now." I'm kidding; I didn't say that last part.

Is there a right answer when describing inkblots? If I said, "The picture on this card is reminiscent of the black-and-white art of the abstract expressionist movement," would that earn me a B+ on the Rorschach test? What if I described the cliffs as two windows into darkness, and the polar bears as Satan's little helpers? Would that have gotten me a diagnosis in high school? Did the psychologist have a sit-down with my parents and say, "Water, two cliffs, and polar bears? She's good."

Mom makes an appointment for me to see her therapist. She's been seeing this therapist for several months. After she started therapy, the phrase "dysfunctional family" entered her vocabulary. Whenever Mom says, "My therapist says," the response from my father is like a tsunami erupting over his eyes.

I tell Mom that I think our family is rather normal (whatever that means) compared to family stories I hear from my friends: "Mom, I think our family is pretty vanilla." Evidently I'm the leading contributor to the family's dysfunction—headline news at the therapist—so I have no room to speak about other families' dysfunctions, other than to share with Mom that my friend John's father was arrested for embezzling five thousand dollars from his company to spend on his wife's brother, with whom he'd been having an affair.

Mom sips on a glass of Metamucil mixed with water—a glaring example of my point.

~

Talk therapy is very beneficial if you have a good therapist. This therapist is not one of them. The therapist starts our session by requesting I list all my male and female personality traits.

What the hell? Aren't you supposed to ask me why I feel the need to self-medicate, or why I'm not working harder toward my future?

I've never given any thought to my male and female qualities. It's like taking a test I haven't studied for.

Then she asks me to recall a difficult childhood memory.

"Well, I wasn't allowed to play in the woods with my neighborhood friends. My father was worried about snakes and ticks. Pretty damn ridiculous, if you ask me."

The therapist stares me down, the way a doctor looks down your throat with that little light.

"I ignored my father because I thought it was the silliest thing I'd ever heard. Plus, I wanted to play in the woods with my friends. One day, I came home covered in mud, 'cause I fell in the creek. So now I'm up the creek with my father. No pun intended."

More staring.

"I sneak in through the back door. The family is watching TV in the den. Dad catches sight of my muddy clothes and hauls me into the den. He's madder than hell. He throws me over his leg and spanks the tarnation out of me. My sisters sit on the couch, laughing. That kind of thing happened a lot. That there is some therapy-worthy material, don't you think?"

"How did that make you feel?"

"Completely humiliated. Also, my butt hurt."

The therapist writes notes. This session cannot end soon enough.

"We're not returning to the therapist," Mom announces one night before an appointment.

"Good. I don't like her. What prompted this decision?"

"She thinks that I'm a lesbian, and that I'm in denial about it. Not that there's anything wrong with being a lesbian—but I'm not." Mom seems nervous to say it.

"What? Can you please find another therapist I can talk to about our therapist?"

Mom writes annual family update letters at Christmas. The letters during my early years say things like, "Kathy has a lot of energy and she loves to laugh. She joined a Girl

Scout Troop. She still takes ballet." During my teen years, the letters say things like, "Kathy is a senior in high school. She's a big fan of the band The Who." That's it. Here's what Mom doesn't add: "We all pray she doesn't die before graduation."

I do graduate from high school—though just barely, after I'm caught smoking pot around the side of the school. Soon everyone knows about it. At that time, there are only two weeks left in the semester. Had I been caught earlier in the year, I could have made the senior superlative list for Most Likely to Secede.

My family throws a "We Can't Believe Kathy Graduated" party.

-3-

The summer of 1983 is unbearably hot, thanks to the three-foot-wide open brick oven in the Colonial Williamsburg bakery where I work. I'm in character, dressed in a white mob hat, peasant blouse, vest, long skirt, apron, and knee-high socks that do nothing to help me keep cool in any way.

The offending oven is located just around the corner from where I sell cookies and apple cider. If I peer around the wall, I can watch an interpreter slide a large metal baking sheet that holds a dozen loaves of bread into its hungry mouth, as he demonstrates colonial baking to a crowd of dripping tourists. The demonstration is held all day long.

Ninety-degree Virginia heat never feels as good as when I exit that bakery.

I spent my senior year of high school in art class, pouring every ounce of my energy into a portfolio for a college art program. I'm passionate about interior design—determined to make it my career.

My father regularly busts my chops about it. "You'll never get a damn job with an art degree," he tells me. This, coming from a man who majored in music.

Blowing off college is partly a middle finger to my father, and partly because school is challenging for me—science and math in particular. The challenge does not help my self-confidence, which is already deficient. The thought of being surrounded by my classmates all day, every day, is exhausting to my introverted spirit.

So now, as summer turns to fall and many of my friends begin their first year of college, I'm working at a pop-up bakery stand in Colonial Williamsburg. Soon the oaks, maples, and walnut trees that line Duke of Gloucester Street are in peak autumn color, a brilliant contrast to the modest colonial homes. No cars are allowed on this street—only horse-drawn carriages, along with interpreters and the occasional fife and drum performers scattered amid the meandering tourists.

I wait inside the pop-up stand for the next customers. A musket shoots off from the gunpowder magazine.

A family of four approaches the stand. The boy dons a tricorn hat and blows into a fife, his fingers tapping along the holes as though he has mastered the instrument in the five minutes since he purchased it. The girl wears a white mob hat and clutches a stick of saltwater taffy.

I sigh, "I love your hats! Can I see them?"

They nod and hand me the hats. I place the tricorn hat on top of my mob hat, then the small mob hat on top of the tricorn hat.

"What do you think?"

Their giggles are as cute as they are.

The whole clan buys gingerbread cookies and apple cider. The girl says, "Aren't you scared of those yellow jackets flying around the apple cider?"

"Nope. I've never once been stung. Can you believe it?"

"Whoa," she mumbles with a mouthful of cookie.

The family stands nearby while they finish their treats. I ask them where they are from, and how they like Williamsburg.

Just then, my best friend Thomas pulls up on the no-vehicles-allowed street, honking the horn of his shiny blue '68 Dodge Coronet, a car that looks like the Batmobile minus the wings.

"Hey, Kathy. Wanna go to a party tonight?"

Oh my God, Thomas, what are you doing? "Okay." I pray my boss is not around.

"I'll pick you up around seven." Thomas pulls off, laying on his horn and scattering tourists in his wake.

I met Thomas in senior year. Our fathers are both college professors, and we're both the youngest children of large, tight-knit families. We're both intellectually curious, self-destructive misfits. We became best buddies at first sight.

Thomas reminds me of the comedian Gallagher—not because he's into smashing watermelons with a mallet like Gallagher does, but because they are both goofballs, and they bear a slight physical resemblance.

Thomas and I are partners in partying. Whether it's a big blowout bash or an intimate gathering of friends, we hang out a lot. One time we stayed out all night. I arrived home before my parents woke up, so I didn't get in trouble. But Thomas' parents didn't sleep because they were worried sick about him. Thomas made up a story about being robbed at gunpoint. He claims he went back to the party afterward and waited until morning to leave.

Thomas' parents called the police. Thomas gave a full description of the nonexistent robber. The incident was published in the local newspaper.

Thomas pulls up in front of my parents' house, honking

his car horn to alert me of his arrival.

I jump in the car. "I can't believe you drove down DOG Street." "DOG" is short for "Duke of Gloucester." "I wish I'd had my camera. You should have seen the looks on the tourists' faces."

"It was big fun."

Thomas and I take a hit of acid. We go to pick up our friend John. We all want to get high, but when I look for my pot, I realize I forgot it at home.

I say, "Let's go to my house. I'll run upstairs. Nobody will notice or care." I'm on the upward escalator already.

I run in the front door of my parents' house to find that my oldest sister and her husband have come for a visit. They're sitting in the den. Cindy is about seven months pregnant. It's the first time I've seen her since she made the announcement.

I walk to the middle of the den and start laughing uncontrollably at the sight of her belly. It's way funnier than it should be. It shouldn't be funny at all. I put my hand over my mouth and say, "I'm sorry. It's just . . . your belly. It's a big ol' belly." The fact that I know I shouldn't be laughing makes everything funnier. I'm making a complete fool of myself. I run out of the room without saying goodbye—I just bolt.

We head to the frat house where the party is being held. The frat brothers are friendly, eccentric guys who are patient with locals hanging around and partying with them.

I take a seat in a frat brother's room. Jeff is a quiet, intense anthropology major. He is nice and easy to be around.

Jeff pulls out a bong. He takes a hit, blows out a cloud of

smoke, coughs, and says, "'Death is our eternal companion. It is always to our left, an arm's length behind us. Death is the only wise adviser that a warrior has.'"

I say, "I'm not a fan of death."

"The fear of death is not the way of the warrior. These are *The Teachings of Don Juan* by Carlos Castaneda."

Another frat guy joins us and takes a bong hit.

I say, "No offense, Jeff, but the death talk is not elevating my buzz."

The new guy says, "I don't know what you're talking about, but I also vote no to the death discussion."

Jeff moves on to discussing Friedrich Nietzsche's philosophy about dream experiences and music while we listen to Sun Ra, an artist whose music sounds like the planets Venus and Saturn took LSD and composed jazz.

Several more frat brothers join us. One of them mentions that the Grateful Dead is playing in Syracuse, New York, tomorrow night. Does anyone want to go? I say, "Sure." Two other frat brothers want to go too. It's one in the morning.

We all pile into the first brother's old yellow Pinto, which I am informed is called The Lemon. We have sixteen hours of driving ahead of us. The driver takes a hit of acid to help him stay awake. In retrospect, the whole thing is as crazy as the opening scene of that movie *Eraserhead.*

Soon enough, we're in the mountains. We've gone through plenty of beer and joints—except for the driver, who is only tripping. One of the frat guys says, "Anyone know what state we're in?" That sets off a bout of uncontrollable laughter in everyone. The driver pulls over at a scenic viewpoint. We all jump out of the car and laugh for about fifteen minutes, holding our legs together so we don't pee.

We have no idea where we are. We go to a gas station. I'm elected to go inside and ask for directions. I stand in line behind a few customers. It's around seven in the morning. I want to feel like a normal human should feel at seven. Like the customers in front of me, purchasing coffee and breakfast.

It takes every ounce of my composure not to lose it. I won't look at The Lemon, because I know I will bust out laughing. Finally, it's my turn with the cashier. It takes all my self-control to say, "Could you please—give me—directions—to Syracuse?"

He gives me the directions.

I say, "Thank you." Then I erupt into the laughter I held in while waiting in line. "Hahahahahahaha!"

I walk to The Lemon and get inside. I say, "I can't remember one word he said."

That causes us all to get out of the car and run around the parking lot, laughing. Customers are staring at us. I walk back in and ask the clerk to write down the directions. He smiles and looks at me as if to say, *I want some of what you're on.*

We make it to Syracuse. It's a damn wonder we didn't end up in Topeka, Kansas. We have several hours to wander around the parking lot of the Syracuse Carrier Dome. The parking lot has already been taken over by Grateful Dead fans listening to music, dancing, and partying. We make friends all over the place. It's a huge party of happy, friendly folks who are very excited that they are going to see the Grateful Dead. It's big fun.

During the concert, I dance. I look around, and suddenly, the guys are nowhere to be seen. I panic. I don't remember where we parked.

Between the lack of sleep and the twenty-four hours' worth of sustained substance abuse, I'm suddenly overcome with a sense of dread as potent as if the Russians had just declared nuclear war.

I sit on a wall and watch people dancing and smiling. I envy them. They are not lost. The concert ends. Fifty thousand concertgoers file past me. I'm there for about ten minutes. Then the guys appear and say, "Oh, hey. There you are."

I cannot believe it. I think, *That's a goddamned miracle.*

We exit the dome. A gust of wind from the pressurized environment gives us a swift push out. We laugh and try to remember where The Lemon is parked. It takes us at least an hour to locate it.

We take turns driving home. At one point, the owner of The Lemon requests we pull over, because he's sick to his stomach. He runs into the woods. When he comes back to The Lemon, he notices one tire is about to fall off. He gets a wrench out of the trunk and tightens the tire. It's another miracle.

℀

In the end, we make it home safe.

I don't know what it is about the Grateful Dead, but that's not the only miraculous scenario that ever occurred in my life in relation to them. Sometime later, Thomas and I go to see them in concert at Merriweather Post Pavilion.

Thomas and I and our friend Mark drive to a brownstone in Washington, DC, to meet up with Mark's friend, who has invited us to stay the night at his place.

Thomas and I get separated from Mark at the show. We hang out in the parking lot. We have no money. We get to talking to an older fellow. Turns out he's a cabdriver. He says he'll give us a ride to DC free of charge. We're driving around the area where we suspect the brownstone is located, but it's a whole neighborhood of brownstones and they all look alike.

The cabdriver stops. Thomas and I get out and wonder what the heck we're going to do. We pick a place at random and knock on the door. It's the right brownstone.

❧

Back in Williamsburg, I embark on a yearlong work-and-party adventure that becomes less adventurous and more mundane as time goes by. I'm in a rut the size of the Grand Canyon, with no exit path in sight.

My friend Audra and I are walking to the frat house's annual '60s party. On the way Audra sees Keep Off the Grass signs on the football field. Audra climbs the fence and takes a sign. We arrive at the party. Audra hands the sign to a frat brother who is getting ready to do a bong hit. He places the sign in the top of his window.

There's a guy at the party who's a Marine. Nobody seems to know him, but I suspect he's taken a lot of something. The Marine is jumping out of a trash can on the porch, yelling, "Who scraped the *J* off your forehead?"

He has a crazy look in his eyes. The college police come and haul him away.

℘

I attend a huge party in the country. I reckon all of young Williamsburg is in attendance. There are multiple bands, a few dozen kegs, and unlimited joints. It's a weekend event.

I pour my first cup of beer. From then on, it's nonstop drinking for me. My goal is to get to a happy place. To feel comfortable talking to people. There is no break in the beer drinking. I'm pounding them down.

The last thing I remember is stepping onto a school bus. I'm unsteady on my feet, and visibly wasted. I need to lie down.

I see the neighborhood punk—more like his asshole father than his sweet mother—and the three guys who are hanging out with him. As I come over, my neighbor puts his hand up my skirt and shoves his fingers up my vagina, the action as aggressive as his character.

I'm in shock. I'm floating in and out of consciousness. I just want to sleep. The guys are laughing. I manage to walk to the back of the bus and pass out.

The next day, I call Thomas and tell him what happened. Thomas is devastated. He spray-paints RAPIST on the neighbor's truck and slashes his tires.

For a while after that, every night when I lie down for bed, I visualize an incident that occurred several years ago.

It's winter. Around six inches of snow has fallen, and all the neighborhood kids have gathered at the top of the street. The main road through Williamsburg lies right in front of us.

My neighbor makes a snowball and dips it in a puddle so that it becomes an ice ball. He kneels down behind a bush and waits for a car to drive by. When one does, he pops up and throws the ice ball as hard as he can onto the driver's side of the windshield. He laughs.

The car turns around and speeds toward him. He runs away, laughing. The driver gets out of the car. He's seething. He says, "He's lucky I didn't catch him. I'd beat the shit out of him."

I envision him getting caught. I envision the man beating the shit out of him.

ᜒ

I'm in my parents' kitchen around midday, after one late-nighter too many. My father walks in from the garage where he is working on his VW Bug with my brother.

"Have you ever thought about joining the military?"

I nearly spit out my coffee.

"Dad, do you really think your war-hating, defiant daughter would last longer than five minutes in the military?"

The phone rings, saving me from my father. Mom says, "Kathy, Thomas is on the phone."

"Hey Kathy, do you want to go see the Grateful Dead in California?"

It sounds much better than joining the military.

"Okay."

I leave a note on the kitchen table for my parents:

"Hi Mom and Dad,

By the time you read this I'll be traveling on a Greyhound Bus to California to see the Grateful Dead. Don't worry about me. I have $188.00 and a sleeping bag.

Love, Kathy"

I'm willing to bet a lot of money my parents will bemoan my inadvertent birth at length after reading my letter. Either that, or they'll rejoice that I'm out of their hair.

Thomas and I are well settled on the Greyhound bus. We're passing through Amarillo, Texas, weaving hundreds of colorful embroidery bracelets that we hope to sell at the Grateful Dead show in Ventura, California. We'll have a lot of competition among the arts-and-crafts vendors that invariably fill the parking lot.

Thomas is weaving bracelets in a frenzy. "The Battle of Chickamauga was the first battle in Georgia, in September 1863. The Confederates won. There were 18,454 Confederate casualties and 16,170 Union losses. It was the second-highest loss after Gettysburg."

There are a few moments of silence. Then Thomas continues.

"There were a hundred and twenty generals at Gettysburg, and nine of them were killed. Nine. That's a lot. Pickett's Charge had around twenty thousand Confederate soldiers, but Gaines' Mill had more than fifty thousand Confederate soldiers."

I weave bracelets like nobody's business. "If I was a soldier, I would run away. I would run away and hide behind a big log. If I had Elmer's glue, I would glue leaves all over my body and lie still, in disguise."

"They didn't make Elmer's glue back then."

"Well, they made some kind of adhesive. It may not have dried clear, but I would make sure I had a bottle for my clever leaf disguise."

Thomas jumps up. "Oh my God, look at that row of

cars with their hoods sticking in the ground." We drop our bracelets, laughing our heads off.

"What do you reckon that's for? What's the point?"

I conclude it's a modern-day junkyard. They're making good use of the space.

We'll later learn that we were driving by Cadillac Ranch, an art installation featuring a row of brightly colored Cadillacs, their hoods pushed into the sand with their trunks in the air. Junk or art, it's the most interesting thing we've seen for hundreds of miles.

Back to weaving.

Thomas says, "When we each get married, we'll still be best friends, no matter what."

I think about marriage. It's a distant notion. "Of course we will. Even if we hate each other's spouses, we'll always be best friends."

Thomas and I arrive in Ventura, California, a swanky beach town that is likely rattled at the sight of thousands of hippies sporting tie-dyes, some of whom like to spin around and blow bubbles. In fact, there is an official group of Grateful Dead fans, otherwise known as Deadheads, called the Spinners. They call themselves the Church of Unlimited Devotion. I think they should be called the Church of Unlimited Spinning. During the concerts, they spin around and around and around for the entire show, like whirling dervishes. Many of them don dresses that balloon out when they twirl.

Every time I see the Spinners, I get dizzy. Even if I wanted to become a member, I couldn't. I'd get sick after two minutes and have to spend the rest of the concert sitting down.

I was twelve years old when I first learned of the Grateful Dead, when I walked out the front door of my parents' house one day and saw the William and Mary Concert Hall through the woods. The parking lot was filled with people wearing colorful tie-dyes. I thought the circus was in town.

It was Parent's Weekend. There were tables of food set up for the parents next to William and Mary Hall. The Deadheads helped themselves. I can imagine a persnickety father, all proud of his smart kid who got accepted to William and Mary, filling a plate with ham biscuits and potato salad when suddenly, a long-haired guy wearing a skirt comes spinning by the food table and says, "Hey, man! Want to hit this joint?"

I figure that's about how it went. All I know is, the Grateful Dead are now banned from playing William and Mary Hall.

Thomas and I approach the county fairgrounds in Ventura. After seventy-two hours of traveling, I'm beyond delighted to exit the bus at last.

"Oh my God, Thomas, Ventura is beautiful. The beach and mountains and palm trees and surfers. It's everything I imagined California to be. Woo-hoo!"

The song "Estimated Prophet" plays in my head:

> *California, preaching on the burning shore*
> *California, I'll be knocking on the golden door*
> *Like an angel, standing in a shaft of light*
> *Rising up to paradise, I know I'm gonna shine.*

After the show, Thomas and I catch a ride with some folks who are traveling up north. We drive through Santa Cruz and up scenic Highway 1 to a beautiful and remote beach called Greyhound Rock, where we join a dozen or so hippies who claim the beach as their temporary home. Below the craggy cliffs crash the wild waves of the Pacific Ocean.

Greyhound Rock is a massive boulder the size of a blue whale. It reigns supreme over the smaller rock formations that dot the shoreline. Elephant seals bask in the sun, sometimes letting out guttural grunts that sound as awkward as the seals look.

Sleeping bags are scattered across the beach that runs along the base of the cliff. Each day, we make the treacherous climb up the cliff to the parking lot and catch a ride to Santa Cruz, where we eat at a soup kitchen and hang around town. We return to the beach in the evenings and party all night.

The vagrant lifestyle gets old quick. I'm around people 24/7. I'm coping with anxiety and depression. I feel like an oddball—and let me just say that if you feel like an oddball around a group of smelly hippies who live on a beach, smoke pot all day, and engage in free-for-all dancing around a bonfire like every evening is a Neolithic summer solstice celebration, you probably have serious issues.

Thomas and I decide to try to hitchhike to San Francisco to see the Jerry Garcia Band. A van pulls over to pick us up. The couple inside are middle-aged and they both smile at Thomas and me. They appear kind. No serial killer vibes.

The woman asks, "Where are you heading?"

Thomas says, "San Francisco."

They both wave their hands. "Hop on in!"

I step up to the rear of the van. The walls are covered with blinking lights and panelboards decked out with knobs. We are catching a ride with two happy Silicon Valley geeks.

I ask what's up with the van. The man says it's a hobby of his during his spare time, when he's not writing code for a living.

I say, "Oh. This is the opposite of my hobbies. Definitely not a Martha Stewart project."

As we approach San Francisco, the woman hands me a piece of paper. She says, "This is my brother's address and phone number. Go stay with him. Tell him I sent you."

After the Jerry Garcia show, we knock on the brother's door. It's about an hour after midnight. He opens the door. "Come on in!" His hospitality is warm. He cooks us breakfast in the morning.

A few weeks pass. One night, I sit alone at the beach camp. Everyone else is sleeping. I'm wide awake and very stoned. The moon is full. I can see figures moving around, but I cannot tell whether they are elephant seals or Charles Manson's cronies, lurching around behind the rocks.

I pretend to be sleeping. I reckon if they are Manson's cronies, they'll kill the sleeping hippies closest to them. I'll sneak behind the big boulder to my left and either find a rock to throw, or run like hell.

೧

The next day, I wake up and wonder why I'm living on a beach with a crew of folks whose main vision of their future involves where to score the next joint.

I return to my parents' home. I'm depressed and wandering aimlessly. I wake up midday, make cheese toast, and sit with my parents and brother while they watch TV: the news; football; *60 Minutes; Murder, She Wrote.*

Mom says, "I just love Angela Lansbury. Did you see how she tracked down that murderer? Goodness, she's one smart gal."

Dad says, "For crying out loud, Phil. It's just a TV show."

Robert is on his second bowl of Breyers Neapolitan ice cream. He's at least a hundred pounds overweight. He scratches at the psoriasis patches on his arms until they bleed.

Two years after leaving his thirty-year career as a hard-working music teacher, band director, and mentor to college kids, my father is not a happy retiree. Now, he is planted in front of the tube for hours. The occasional swing jazz gig is a welcome respite, but he returns home to his pain-in-the-ass daughter and a life that, to him, must be about as interesting as the song "I Write the Songs" by Barry Manilow.

Hoo, boy. I love my family, but I need to get the heck out of there. I apply for waitressing jobs, and hope for a much more pleasant experience than the one I had during my first and only foray into the restaurant game to date.

The first restaurant in question was The Lafayette. It was my first day. Everything was going well. I got the dinner orders for a large party correct. I brought the food to the table without incident. Then I returned to refill their waters. The ice had settled into a giant ice cube on the bottom of the pitcher. I had no prior water pitcher experience, so I was ignorant of the imminent danger.

The giant ice cube came gushing out all over a lady's plate of *saganaki*. I was mortified. Unsure what to say, I opted for humor: "Guess you're having *soggy-naki* for dinner! Ha-ha!"

The owner ran over and screamed at me in Greek with a few choice English words thrown into the mix, like "idiot" and "klutz." The customers laughed at the spectacle. I ran out the back door—and thus ended my two-hour tenure.

❧

It's the fall of 1985. My friend Kevin calls to invite me to see a Grateful Dead cover band in Richmond, Virginia, about an hour away from my hometown. I have no idea there is such a thing as Grateful Dead cover bands. We spend the day in Richmond, exploring the James River and the beautiful, historic homes.

I fall in love with the city. Within a week, I find a room to rent in a turn-of-the-century house located around the corner from Monument Avenue, a six-mile-long drag lined with hundred-year-old trees and nineteenth-century mansions with beautiful gardens. Statues of Confederate generals tower in the wide, grassy median strips that divide the regal avenue. A walk along Monument Avenue in springtime is a visual wonder of flowering dogwoods, redbuds, phlox, and tulips.

Mom calls with news that my sister gave birth. "Cindy had a boy. He weighs eleven pounds and four ounces, and he was born breech. It was very painful, but everyone is fine and healthy."

"Whoa," I say. "An eleven-pounder born breech? That's a whole lot of nope." Mom responds with an obligatory chuckle.

"I'll never forget your birth. Goodness, it was awful."

"How so?"

"Oh, I don't remember the details." Mom is comfortable with her routine amnesia.

I get a similar answer to most questions about my childhood. It makes filling out medical history forms an adventure. *"Hey, Mom, did I ever have chicken pox?" "Honey, I got all you kids mixed up, with who had what disease when. Of course I don't remember."*

On the phone, she continues: "Something went wrong with the stirrups. All I remember is that it was terrible." She laughs nervously. I think, *You laugh, but Miss Possibly-Brain-Damaged-Daughter over here doesn't think it's so funny.*

As I hang artwork in my new apartment, a friendly fellow appears at my door. "Hey. I'm Ray. I live down the hall. Just wanted to introduce myself. We can hang out later if you want."

Ray has dark hair that falls down his neck. He reminds me of a character from the movie *The Outsiders*, trying to get his act together.

I take Ray up on the offer. He plays one of my favorite songs on his turntable—Bob Dylan's "It's Alright, Ma (I'm Only Bleeding)." Ray and I talk for hours about his four older siblings, his alcoholic father, and growing up poor. What Ray was denied in his troubled upbringing, he makes up for with a great sense of humor.

Being with Ray is like sitting in a hot tub on a cool evening. A month after we meet, we move into a one-bedroom apartment together. Between his construction job and my work as a waitress, we're poor; but we're wealthy in our adventures: hiking along the river, visiting parks, hanging out with friends, listening to music, and visiting our families.

Around five or six months into our relationship, Ray and I are strolling along Monument Avenue. Ray has his arm around me. He says, "Hey, babe." I can tell he's nervous. "Do you want to get married?"

I'm twenty-one years old, and everything is moving along faster than a Porsche on the German Autobahn. *Holy moly, I don't know,* I think. *Can't we just date a while longer?* But instead of saying, "I think it's too soon," I say, "Okay." I'm a mess and a misfit. Ray loves me, and for that I am grateful.

We get married less than a year after we first met—although my second thoughts are so brutal, they reduce me to tears. I want to call off the wedding, but I cannot bear to do it.

Two months later—in keeping with our trend of moving along fast—I'm pregnant with our daughter, Melissa. I get a job as a receptionist at a small mailing services company.

Melissa is born in October of 1986.

One beautiful spring day in May, I arrive home from work to find Thomas has unexpectedly come to visit. Ray is chatting with him. They've hit it off immediately.

"Oh my God, Thomas!" We embrace.

Thomas looks awful. He's gaunt, and his color is not good. I'm fairly certain he's using hard drugs.

Thomas is taking a break from the Grateful Dead tour. He stays with us for several weeks. I don't know it at the time, but Thomas is coming down from a daily heroin habit while he stays with us. He tells us he thinks he has the flu.

Ray and I barely get by on the money we earn. Now we

have the added expense of a seven-month-old baby. I decide it's time to plan for a different career. The question is, what do I want to do?

ↄ

My family still gathers every summer at the beach in the Outer Banks—the seven of us, plus spouses and kids. I'm engaged in a lovely conversation with my sister, Cindy, the eldest of the clan.

The Atlantic Ocean is in a powerful mood. We sip wine and watch waves crashing like bolts of thunder. Whitecaps dot the surface beyond the shoreline.

I love these family gatherings. My relationship with my siblings has aged well. There is no other place I want to be.

Cindy is a rock. My sisters and I listen to her advice like its gospel.

Cindy mentions she has a friend who is a paralegal. The money is decent, and the job market is good. I should consider it as a career, she says.

Then she asks me about Dad. I live closer to our parents than Cindy does, so I visit them more often. Cindy says, "Dad seems out of it, and depressed. Maybe it's just postretirement blues, but I wonder if it could be dementia."

I also notice that Dad is getting absentminded. The last time I visited my parents, he walked over to the kitchen table, fumbling through the stack of mail. "Did I get any mail?" He'd already asked the question five minutes before.

"No, Chuck." Mom's patience resonates each time she responds.

I look up at the beach house, where Dad is sitting in a

rocking chair. He's dressed in slacks, a casual dress shirt, and suspenders. It's his everyday outfit, not his usual beach attire. His olive face is chiseled, long and thin against the bright white boards that circle behind him. His dark brown eyes are modest. Authority is replaced with vulnerability. The laugh lines have moved above his eyes.

I wrap a beach towel around my shoulders. Cindy does the same. We pour another glass of wine and sit in silence, watching the mighty Atlantic Ocean.

Our sisters Sara and Kris appear behind the half-circle of beach chairs where Cindy and I sit, breaking the silence of ocean gazing.

"We brought more wine." Then, a round of Chardonnay and pure joy.

The tide changes.

-4-

I take Cindy's advice and sign up for night school, in an effort to earn a paralegal degree. Before I begin classes, I take a math placement test. They want me to divide fractions. Afterward, the college places me in a class I call "Math for Dummies."

To get through school, I purchase a supplement similar to speed—but it's all-natural. I call it "Get Shit Done." I drink boatloads of coffee.

I get a job at a law office while I'm in school. The five attorneys who practice there take whatever type of case they can get their hands on. Being a lawyer is a competitive gig.

John specializes as a criminal defense attorney. He is so shady, I wonder whether he might need to defend himself one day. His Ralph Lauren blazer says "schmuck" the same way Danny Zuko's leather jacket proclaims him "cool."

My marriage disintegrates to a point that's about as healthy as pizza and beer, without the "going together" part. After a long run of trying to make it work, Ray and I decide to separate. We strive for civility during the process. It's a challenge, but it mostly works.

A few weeks after the separation Ray tells me about all the things that are going wrong with his new apartment. While I'm at work, I listen to Jeff and Jeff, a couple of pranksters from a local radio station. The segment is called

"Victim of the Day." They call unsuspecting victims and play practical jokes on them.

I had pranked Ray via the show once before. One day, listening to Jeff and Jeff, I get the idea to prank Ray a second time.

I call the radio station. One of the Jeffs immediately remembers Ray, because his reaction to being pranked the first time was loud and scattered with expletives. Jeff tells me Ray is their favorite Victim of the Day.

I tell Jeff that Ray and I recently separated, and that I have an idea for a prank.

Jeff is worried. "Hmm. What do you have in mind?"

"He recently moved into an apartment. He told me a list of things wrong with the place. He just dropped off the list with the landlord."

I give Jeff the list of problems. He rolls with it.

One of the Jeffs (the other one) calls Ray and pretends to be the landlord. Jeff sounds like a schmucky used car salesman. "I'd like to go over the list of the problems in your apartment."

Ray says, "Okay."

Jeff says, "Regarding the worn-out and damaged tile in the kitchen, I've arranged for you to pick up a used piece of tile from a veterinarian's office in Dinwiddie."

Ray says, "Uh-huh."

Jeff: "You say you've got to manually turn the lightbulb in the bathroom to make it work? I suggest you don't stand in the bathtub while you turn on that lightbulb."

Ray: "Uh-huh."

Jeff: "Let's see here . . . the cracked window. My advice

is that you stay away from that window. By the way, the neighbors tell me they saw you with a potbellied pig. We don't allow potbellied pigs in the building."

Ray remains polite, but it's obvious he's seething. "You mean to tell me you want me to pick up a used piece of tile from a veterinarian's office to replace my kitchen tile, not stand in the bathtub when I turn on the lightbulb, and stay away from the cracked window? You have got to be kidding me. And by the way, I don't own a potbellied pig; it's a pit bull."

"Ray. This is Jeff and Jeff. You're Victim of the Day."

"OH MY GOD, OH MY GOD! YOU GUYS SUCK! Ha-ha, ha-ha! You guys suck! You really got me good."

ᏉᎧ

After I graduate from college, I land a job as a corporate paralegal. On my first day, I meet Nancy, the lawyer I'm assigned to assist. The department she represents refers to her as "Narcy," because she is a raging narcissist.

I reckon Nancy is around thirty years old. She tells me she earned an MBA before she went to law school, and that her student loans cost more than her mortgage. Then she tells me she was supposed to be valedictorian of her high school class, but there was a tie. The school picked another student over her. "I was salutatorian only because the school made a bad decision."

It's a good thing she clears that up, because I had totally been judging Nancy by her salutatorian status. Nancy is clearly good at holding a long-term grudge.

Nancy requests I create a contract. After I bring her the

first draft, she returns it to me and says, "This box here needs to be a third of an inch smaller." I make the change and send it along. Again, she brings it back. "Remove this box." I show her the revised document. "Actually, put the box back, but remove *this* box." The drafting of the one-page contract goes on for an entire day.

Jesus Christ, I think. My mind is no day in the park, but I would seriously hate to be inside Nancy's head.

Day after day, we work on contracts. It's brutal. If there is a more uptight lawyer anywhere in the world, I never want to work for them.

ల

After a particularly rough day, I decide to go to a drum circle I attend every so often. Perhaps beating on a drum will calm my frustrations.

The drum circle is a meeting of percussionists who gather at a city park facility called the Round House, an aptly named facility that's appropriate to the group's circular theme. Depending on the drummers in attendance, the circle sometimes sounds like the percussion section of a Santana concert. At other times, it sounds like the drum section of a first-grade band.

After tonight's drum circle, I chat with Wayne, a long-time member of the group. He is one of the Santana-worthy percussionists. He shares his trail mix with me.

On New Year's Eve, my friend Meg and I go out to see the Ululating Mummies, a fun, multicultural band of creative misfits that plays danceable songs with titles like "Lebanese Hillbilly Music" and "Dance of the Bird

People." They dress up in flashy robes and wear weird hats. The saxophone player, Danny, makes his hats out of colorful kids' pants, stuffing the legs so that they perch upon his head in whimsical glory.

I tell Meg I have a feeling I'm going to meet someone that night. The proclamation comes after three beers and a shot of wishful thinking.

The Ululating Mummies' show is packed. I have a happy buzz when I arrive. George, the bass clarinet player, has his face wrapped up like a mummy. I later find out it's the anniversary of his wife's death. The gauze masks the uncontrollable tears that pour down his face all night long.

I see Wayne at the show. We dance to the groovy sounds of the accordion, saxophone, bass clarinet, drums, bass, and guitar. We hang out during the set break. Wayne reigns nearly a foot over my five-foot-two frame, and I like it. He has long, silky auburn hair; long sideburns; and a nice smile. I recall how friendly he was at the drum circle. I'm smitten.

Next thing you know, we're kissing each other. Then more, and more. We are surrounded by people. PDA is not my thing, but all my inhibitions vanished several beers ago.

My friend Meg leaves after the midnight countdown. Wayne and I continue our dance party. Then he gives me a ride home.

When we get there, I say, "Wayne, I can't find my key."

"We can go to my house," he offers.

"No, I have to get inside. My dog needs me. See if you can break through the French doors on the porch."

Wayne pushes and kicks the doors. A guy walking by on the sidewalk turns to look, and I say, "Happy New Year" like everything is kosher.

The tenant that lives to the left of me turns on his light while Wayne is making all this racket. Wayne and I get inside. My dog, Maggie, is overjoyed to see me.

I hear a loud knock at the front door. At first, I think it's an irritated neighbor coming to complain about the noise—but instead, it's three police officers.

"Ma'am, are you okay?"

"Yes, Officers. I had to break into my apartment. Sorry for the trouble."

I tell Wayne I'm going to bed. I have to get up early. Ray and I are traveling to Georgia tomorrow to visit some good friends.

Wayne knows Ray from the drum circle. I think he knows we are separated. Wayne looks confused. I want to add, "We're not together anymore," but it's an awkward moment.

I don't expect to hear from Wayne again after that fiasco, but to my surprise, he calls to ask me out to dinner. I want to get straight to business, but the line of questions would be far too presumptuous. *Any current girlfriends? How many? Thoughts about children—I mean, not the two of us having children, but children in general? I have one of those. I'm interested in an exclusive relationship. but if that's not your thing, that's no problem at all.*

I'm nervous. The last date I went on took place roughly four score and seven years ago. New Year's Eve with the Ululating Mummies doesn't count. This is my chance to redeem myself.

On this date, I learn that Wayne majored in history in college. The degree is not serving him over and above the knowledge gained. He's studying for a graduate degree in computer programming—the statistics class is killing him. He plays bass in a couple bands: a jazzy singer-songwriter group, and a trio inspired by the music of the Velvet Underground.

We talk about music; the genius of Salvador Dali; our favorite art museums; and the delicious appetizer we ordered, which we deduce contains tomato paste, chili powder, and garlic. The rest of the ingredients are a mystery. Wayne tells me about a street vendor he visited when he studied in Beijing. He says the dumplings were like butter.

Wayne is soft-spoken. I wonder whether he's been through a tragic breakup, and is protecting his vulnerable, broken heart.

Wayne introduces me to his parents. When we come to visit, his mother, Margaret, is walking through her backyard with binoculars, looking at birds in the large stand of trees beyond the fence. She's a short, stout, jolly-looking woman, wearing a hoodie that bears the name of the Audubon society for which she serves as president.

She walks over to the deck to greet us. "Hi, David!" I sense she has a deep affection for her only child, and I wonder why the heck she is calling him David.

"Mom, this is Kathy."

Margaret says hello; it's a bit dismissive. I wonder if she has met so many girlfriends that she's growing tired of it.

I admire her beautiful Cape Cod house, which Wayne's grandfather built in the 1940s. Margaret designed an addition, drawing up the plans herself even though she has no architectural background. I've never seen so many book-shelves—or books—in a house.

Wayne's father arrives home from his job as an attorney. He's a large, tall, reserved man who communicates that he is pleased to meet me with his warm smile.

Wayne's parents suggest we go out to dinner, where Margaret clears up the David/Wayne name discrepancy. "David's name is David Wayne, Jr. There was another student named David in David's class in elementary school. In order to avoid confusion, David agreed to be called Wayne, but he's always been David to us."

I say, "That was considerate of Wayne."

Wayne's father, who is officially called Wayne, asks, "What did I do?"

Should I switch gears in a show of solidarity? *David and I had so much fun last night!*

I'm feeling anxious about the ridiculous name situation, so I try to clear it up while we wait for our dinner to arrive. "Wayne introduced himself to me as Wayne. Wayne is one syllable; David is two syllables. Wayne, Wayne, Wayne. Rolls right off the tongue."

I'm challenging their commitment to the more compli-cated two-syllable name. I'm probably not earning first-im-pression points.

Wayne's father says, "I'm reading the *Personal Memoirs of Ulysses S. Grant.* He was a gifted writer. I consider him the greatest general of all time. He won the first major Union victory—"

Margaret cuts him off. "Wayne, no one wants to hear this."

I say, "My best friend Thomas' father is an authority on the Civil War. He was an expert on the Old South"

Margaret says, "Oh, really? What's his name?"

"Boyd Coyner."

Margaret says, "*The* Boyd Coyner?"

I'm excited. "Yes!"

"Never heard of him before." She grins and turns to her husband, Wayne. "Time to go."

Wayne's parents leave to attend a Democratic Committee meeting.

℘

The next day, I visit my parents. "Hi, Dad. How are you doing?"

Dad answers with a grin: "Sitting up and taking nourishment. That's about it." He has not lost his sense of humor.

By now, my father is experiencing full-blown dementia. Mom is the most patient caretaker he could have.

I take a seat on the couch next to him to watch a football game. For as long as I can remember, Dad reserved every Sunday of the season to watch a game. Robert is his constant companion.

Now, Dad is confused. "I can't keep up with all the commotion on the field. What's happening?" Dad's eyes wander around the den, as though he is searching for a device that will help him comprehend the game. Robert is happy to assume this role as the eager commentator, proud to fill Dad in on the details.

Dad walks over to the coffeemaker. He never makes coffee in the evening. He pulls out the used filter and places it on the kitchen counter. Wet grounds spill into a sloppy mess.

Dad pulls a clean filter from a bag and places it in the pot. He stares at it for a long moment. Eventually he summons Mom.

"Phil, how the hell does this coffeemaker work?"

Dad's shame is heartbreaking to witness.

&

Mom and I sit at the kitchen table. "How are you doing, Mom? It must be difficult taking care of Dad."

"It's not so bad. He's just absentminded, and he repeats questions a lot. Could be worse. Speaking of which, Cindy called me yesterday. She just found out she has breast cancer. She is seeing the best doctors at Johns Hopkins, though, so don't worry. Treatment has come a long way." I detect fear through Mom's mask of resilience.

I want to say to Mom, *You know, you could lose your cool right now due to the pressure of taking care of Dad, Robert's struggles, and learning your firstborn has cancer. You could say, 'Fuck this shit,' and you'd get a pass. Even though it would shock me to kingdom come, bring it on; let it all out. It cannot do you any good bottling up your feelings. One day, they are going to explode like a shaken can of cola.*

Mom used to tell me she respected my ability to express myself. That's one way of putting it. Some would compare my honest expressions to the eruption of Mount St. Helens. But I do think Mom struggles with her inability to express her emotions.

I return home to find a letter from Mom in the mailbox. She includes a letter I recently mailed to her. I write letters to Mom on a regular basis. She often returns them to me with comments and corrections: "It may sound better if you word this paragraph like this."

I contemplate whether or not to call Wayne. Maybe I should wait for him to call me. I'd like to see him. Dating is exhilarating and distressing at the same time.

I'm falling hard for Wayne, and it terrifies me. He may be searching for the right girl—someone who does not have a young child to contend with. Someone who has her life together. I know that isn't me.

In fact, I'm starting to worry that it never will be.

Dad

Mom

My neighborhood partner in fun and me

Vacation in the Outer Banks, NC

Me, circa 1982

Me, circa 1984

Audra (left) and me

Robert

Dad with his grandson, Russell

From left: Kris, Cindy, Sara, me, and Robert

Me in Nine Mile, JA with Bob Marley's uncle, Lloyd

From left: Me, Melissa, Charlie, Megan (Thomas' wife), and Thomas

-5-

Wayne and I have been dating about two-and-a-half years. It's the summer of 1999. Wayne lives in an apartment on the second level of his parents' house. He asks me if I want to do psychedelic mushrooms.

It's been years since I took psychedelic drugs. I'm a mother. My initial reaction is, "No way," but I say, "Okay," because I suck at saying no.

Wayne makes hot tea with the mushrooms. He says, "The guy I bought them from told me to be careful. They're potent."

We each drink a cup of the mushroom tea.

We're sitting on Wayne's couch. I'm so high that I think, *If I get any higher, I might lose my shit.*

We decide to take a walk through the neighborhood. We walk along a path through the woods. I see an old house. There's a beekeeping operation going on. I worry the bees might suddenly attack us—that they might detect our mushroom buzz and get freaked out.

The trees are glowing a fluorescent green. The leaves are breathing. These mushrooms are definitely potent. I think, *What if I never come down?*

We return to Wayne's apartment. He puts on an album. We sit on his couch and lean back with our eyes closed.

The music immediately swallows my mind whole. We're listening to "Spanish Key" by Miles Davis. The heady keyboards, trumpet, saxophone, guitar, and bass clarinet meld into what I think must be the most brilliant music I've ever heard, until I'm sucked into the sonic kaleidoscope party dancing around in my head.

Wayne's father yells up, loud enough for us to hear him over the music, startling us out of our daze.

"Your mother is having heart pain. She thinks she is having a heart attack. I'm taking her to the emergency room."

We both mouth to each other, *Oh my God. What the fuck?*

Wayne's father requests that Wayne sit by the telephone. Wayne takes a Thorazine pill. It helps bring him down. Wayne's friend who works at a pharmaceutical company gave it to him on a recent visit. I wonder if his friend was like, "Here's some Thorazine, just in case you have a psychotic break."

I don't know what to say, so I end up saying, "Well, this is a giant buzzkill." It's the opposite of empathetic.

Finally, we get a call that Wayne's mother is okay. *Phew.*

I haven't done psychedelics since then.

❧

I decide I can't take any more of the corporate law job, and begin to peruse ads for paralegal jobs. One catches my attention: "Paralegal for City Attorneys Who Represent the Department of Social Services."

I apply and get the job. During the interview with the head-honcho city attorney, I ask what the job entails. He says, "You know, social service cases. That kind of thing."

No shit, Sherlock; that's what the ad says. But I hate corporate law so much that I don't care. I'm desperate for a different job, away from Salutatorian Nancy. I want to salute Nancy goodbye.

I arrive for my first day on the job. The office is located in the juvenile court building where the cases are heard. The walk through the waiting area is a visual spectacle. I've always assumed that defendants in court dress conservatively to try to make a good impression, but it soon becomes clear that this is not the case. *Honey, I can see the entirety of your boxer shorts like they are an accessory. They should be an accessory after the fact—like when you pull up your pants.*

I walk into the office just as an attorney comes running through the front door. "You're the new paralegal?" She runs into her office and grabs some papers, hands them to me, and says, "Here, answer these interrogatories. Gotta run back into court."

My new attorney is a fifty-something-year-old badass. Before this, she was working on the North Slope in Alaska, until her coworkers encouraged her to go to law school. She got her law license when she was in her forties. She's got a great sense of humor, and she's smart as a whip.

I make my way to my desk, where I sit down and review the interrogatories. That's when I realize this job mostly involves people who do very bad things to children. On a scale of one to ten in terms of "bad," the case in my hands is a twenty-five.

(Several years later, I attend the attorney's wedding. She introduces me to her husband and says, "I gave Kathy the worst case I've ever seen on her first day on the job. I don't know what I was thinking.")

A speaker above my desk announces, "ALL PARTIES IN THE BROWN CASE, REPORT TO COURTROOM TWO. ALL PARTIES IN THE BROWN CASE, REPORT TO COURTROOM TWO." *Okay, that's a little distracting.* The drone of the speaker goes on all day long.

After work, Wayne comes to visit me to see how my first day went. I collapse on my bed and sob uncontrollably.

"Oh my God, what happened?"

"Dead baby. That's all I can say." Then more sobbing.

I return the next day, even though I want to run away screaming. It's impossible to keep up with all the work. Most of the cases involve child neglect—kids left without enough food or with hygiene issues; single mothers with multiple children, substance abuse problems, mental health issues, etc. Then a case that throws me to my knees comes down the pike.

Until I got the job, I'd thought maybe two people in this town did heroin. Boy, was I wrong. The photos I see of homes in deplorable condition make my house look like Felix Unger from *The Odd Couple* moved in.

I meet child protective service workers when they wait in our office for their cases to be called.

"Hi. I'm Katrina."

Katrina looks like a lady of the night. She's wearing a skirt so short I can almost see her bum, a top that shows her ample cleavage, leopard-print tights, four-inch plat-form heels, and inch-long bright-red fake fingernails with fancy white swirls. If Katrina came to my home to remove my children, I would lock the door and call the police. Apparently it's not just the defendants who missed the memo about how to dress for court.

A few weeks into the job, a guy hops up on the edge of my desk. He's eating cheese nabs, and crumbs are falling on the stack of medical records I'm reviewing. He's wearing jeans with motorcycle boots up to his knees. His hair is greasy, and he smells like a mixture of mildew and Beefaroni. A large pink plastic flower ring is perched on his index finger.

I'm annoyed. "May I help you?"

"I'm waiting for my case to be called."

"There's a waiting area out in the hallway."

"The social workers wait in here."

I'm open-minded about appearances, but this guy is going into homes to remove children, and he presents like Randle McMurphy from *One Flew Over the Cuckoo's Nest*—except not as well-dressed.

Later, one of the attorneys, a woman named Katie, returns from court.

I say, "I met a very interesting social worker today."

"Yeah," she chuckles. "I was just in court with him. One time I caught him in my office on his knees, sniffing my chair. Word at social services is that he steals women's clothing from the homeless donation box and cross-dresses in them."

"What?"

"He leaves me sticky notes all the time. One of them said, 'Leave Muscles. Love, Brains.' 'Muscles' refers to my husband."

"Holy moly."

I suspect it's difficult to find quality social workers for this department. The caseload is three times higher than that of any other jurisdiction in the area. For work that entails firsthand observations of the worst of humanity, the pay is squat.

Katie tells me that the social workers' supervisors won't hire anyone smarter than themselves, for fear of losing their jobs. I know one thing for sure: there is an epidemic of wacky. And my threshold for wacky is higher than Everest.

After work, I go home and drink. Not to the point of inebriation, but more than I should on a daily basis. It softens the blow of my brutal eight-hour day. I know I'm too sensitive for the job, but I want to soldier on.

◈

In 2001 Wayne and I are headed to a concert on the waterfront in Norfolk. We stop to visit Dad on the way. By now, my father has been living at a nursing home for a few years. Mom took good care of him, but she's getting older too, and he needs more help now than she can give him.

Although I don't know it at the time, this will be the only time Wayne ever meets my father. I wish they had met in his prime. They could have talked jazz and Sony D5 recorders. Instead, Wayne's first and only impression of my father is one of an old man holding onto the metal headboard of his bed, a look of terror on his face.

I take his hand. "Dad, I'm on my way to Norfolk. Remember when you used to play your saxophone on the waterfront with the swing jazz band?"

I mention the band leader, and Dad's eyes light up. Music was his life. It's the last shimmering memory in his shattered mind.

I pray that Dad's head is filled with the sounds of Beethoven and Count Basie—and not with the moans that can be heard around the building, or the sounds of the workers who are putting dishes away in the kitchen. The crashing of dishes is a frightening sound for someone who has lost his mind.

As I sit with Dad, I decide that if I owned a convalescent facility, I would play Glenn Miller and dance the jitterbug. I would spray lavender-and-rose perfume and place giant vases filled with Shasta daisies everywhere. I would feed the residents healthy food and tell them bad jokes. Instead of chocolate cake, I would give them blueberry and strawberry smoothies for dessert. They would hate me for that.

As I drive back to Richmond, I get pulled over by a police officer. He says, "Ma'am, do you know how fast you were going?"

I say, "No, sir." I think the speed limit here is sixty-five miles per hour. Unbeknownst to me, it's actually fifty-five.

The officer says, "Seventy-two miles per hour."

I say, "I thought I was going faster than that"—because, assuming as I do that the speed limit here is sixty-five miles per hour, seventy-two does not seem like speeding.

When I go to court, the judge asks the officer if I cooperated with him.

He says, "Yes, your honor. In fact, she said she thought she was going faster than she was."

The entire courtroom busts out laughing.

☙

The visit with my father takes an emotional toll on me.

I'm not sure why. I've visited him many times. I know what to expect.

Later, I discover why I'm such an emotional wreck. Turns out I'm pregnant.

I have no clue how Wayne will take the news.

Wayne comes over to my house. After supper we relax in the bedroom. I say to Wayne, "Hey, I'd like to talk about something."

Wayne tries to hide the panic in his face, as he does every time I say we need to talk about something. It never quite works. I try to be gentle and lead up to the news—but instead, I come out with it at ninety miles per hour. "I'm pregnant."

"You are?"

Wayne reaches over and holds me, and runs his fingers through my hair. He says, "Do you want to get married?"

I vowed never to marry again, but I say yes. I need an intensive course on How to Say No. This would be the one lesson: *It's Not That Difficult; You Just Say No.* The End.

⇛

Back in the office, I trudge through cases. An attorney asks whoever is listening: "Do you smell something foul?"

I'm the sensitive, pregnant Detector of Odors. I say, "Oh my God, yes."

The attorney gets down on her hands and knees, crawling around the office. After a few minutes' sniffing, she comes out of the receptionist's office. The receptionist was fired a week before.

"Found it." She is holding a coffee mug at arm's length.

"It's a mug full of old pee." I guess the three-hundred-pound receptionist was too lazy to walk down the hall to the bathroom.

The attorney walks out the front door and immediately returns.

"What did you do with it?"

"I placed it under the court Christmas tree. I didn't know where else to put it."

Everyone busts out laughing.

☙

The family assembles at Cindy's house for the annual Christmas gathering. Cindy's abdomen is distended. She looks ravaged from chemotherapy. No one is discussing the prognosis, but by my observation, it's not looking good.

Wayne and I marry on New Year's Eve that year. It's the anniversary of our first kiss. The ceremony is held where we met at the Round House. Instead of a drum circle, an intimate circle of family and friends gather around for the ceremony.

Cindy is too ill to attend the wedding. I think about Cindy and her husband, Paul's wedding, many years before. Cindy replaced the wedding vow to "love, honor, and obey" with "love, honor, and Old Bay." Cindy vowed to season all of Paul's meals with that famous blend of eighteen herbs and spices.

My friend Scott, who has a dark sense of humor, shows up in a black suit, and wearing shades. It's how he dresses for every wedding—like he's in mourning for the institution of marriage.

Wayne and I are away on our honeymoon when I receive the news that Cindy has passed away. She was forty-eight years old, a wife and mother of three children, ages eighteen, fifteen, and eleven.

My sisters were by Cindy's side during her final days, while she received hospice care at home. A harpist played music from Cindy's favorite album. It was a peaceful passing.

When I arrive at the church, a brilliant double rainbow stretches across the sky. Cindy's eleven-year-old daughter Erin is in the church lobby, looking sad and overwhelmed. I wish it were a Sunday church service and not her mother's funeral we are attending.

Cindy's husband and sons mingle with familiar faces, distracted by the busy protocol of a funeral service. The following weeks and months after all the formal events are over will be really tough for the family.

At the conclusion of the service, Paul walks up to Cindy's urn. Paul and Cindy were college sweethearts, together for many years. The urn is placed in the center of the church crossing, surrounded by beautiful lilies, graceful and refined like Cindy herself. Paul collapses to his knees, places his hands over his face, and wails. His entire body is shaking.

Then he stands up and collects himself to mingle with friends and family at the reception.

I'll never forget it.

∾

I'm at work. Files are heaped on my desk, overflow stacked on the floor. Death and grief are new experiences for me.

I worry about Cindy's family, and about Mom, who has

just lost her firstborn and is still trying to cope with my father's illness.

My sister Sara's number blinks on my work phone. When I pick up, Sara is in tears. "Dad's breathing is labored. They told us to come right away." It's eleven days after Cindy's death.

My coworkers are very supportive. "Go, now."

As I go to bid farewell to my father, I find myself driving on the same interstate that we used to take in his '69 VW Bug to go shopping at Montgomery Ward. In my memory, Dad says, "C'mon, kid, we're going to Monkey Ward's."

I'm ten years old. I love the shopping trips. While we travel on the interstate Dad talks on his CB radio. "Back off the hammer and don't feed the bears."

I think back to one of Dad's concert band performances that I attended when I was eight years old. The band is seated in a half circle. They're dressed in formal black attire. An important event is unfolding on the stage.

Dad appears through the side curtain, all spiffy in his black tails. The audience shows its approval with loud applause. I raise my hands together as high as they can go. I'm the most enthusiastic clapper in the house.

Dad bows, steps up to the platform, and raises his baton. The band raise their instruments, and erupt into *Fanfare for the Common Man*.

Dad is such a powerful presence. I'm proud to be his daughter.

I remember the first poem I ever wrote:

The water flows down the stream
Under rocks
Over rocks
Some are covered in moss
Others are an unblemished grey
The stream is not slowed by the thick tree root
That snakes in and out of the sodden earth
Or the rotting log that rests halfway between
It flows freely
To the still lake
That soothes my troubled soul

At fourteen years old, I'm eager for Dad's approval. He tells me he likes it.

It's the most important opinion I receive on my poem.

I remember when I was nineteen years old. I'm freaking out at a Grateful Dead concert at Hampton Coliseum. I've been to their concerts, so I figure I know what to expect, and take a hit of acid.

Soon I realize I'm not having a good time. I cannot handle watching the dancers near me. A shirtless, long-haired guy in a tie-dyed skirt spins around and weaves his cupped hands above his head like a blitzed-out belly dancer. Then he scoops them toward the floor and makes circles with them to the beat of the music.

I've seen similar scenes at other Grateful Dead shows, but this time, it's the most bizarre thing I've ever witnessed. I think, *I've got to get out of here immediately. These people are crazy!*

I run through the parking lot until I see a phone booth. I call Dad and beg him to pick me up.

Dad picks me up. He has no idea I'm tripping. He says, "How 'bout we go to Monkey Ward's?" The last thing I want to do is go to Monkey Ward's, but I don't want to raise any suspicions, so I agree.

The lights in the store are blindingly bright. I'm pretty sure all the customers and staff know I'm on acid, and they are staring at me.

Dad wanders around the electronics section. Multiple TV screens are lit up, adding to the over-stimulation of the situation. I cannot wait to leave. We finally leave after Dad has carefully inspected the Sony turntables.

The thirty-minute drive home seems to take hours. Making conversation with a parent while tripping on acid is challenging, but I manage not to mention to Dad that I can see a line of fluorescent baby elephants doing somersaults in the emergency lane.

Back in the present, I arrive at the nursing home. I hold Dad's hands and kiss him on his forehead. He is beyond ready to be released from his ailing existence.

There are no words to describe saying goodbye to a parent. Death is number one on the list of life's stressors. I think it deserves its own list, titled "There Are No Words."

I'm relieved that Cindy will be on the other side to greet him after our send-off. Her beautiful smile will comfort him.

ఌ

I'm graveside with the family after the funeral service.

It's pouring down rain, a deluge to match the tears streaming down my face.

The family is gathered in a circle around Dad's grave. The minister speaks his final words. Suddenly, Dad's jazz band buddies break into a Dixieland-style version of "When the Saints Go Marching In" under a large, dripping oak tree. I don't have any tears left to shed.

Two months after Cindy's and Dad's passings, I discover there's a serious medical issue with my pregnancy. I lose the baby.

I'm emotionally wiped. Denial is the elixir to my despair, alcohol the sloppy bandage.

Kahlil Gibran's *The Prophet* sits on my nightstand. I pick it up and read:

"For what is it to die but to stand naked in the wind and to melt into the sun? And what is it to cease breathing but to free the breath from its restless tides, that it may rise and expand and seek God unencumbered? Only when you drink from the river of silence shall you indeed sing. And when you have reached the mountaintop, then you shall begin to climb. And when the earth shall claim your limbs, then shall you truly dance."

It's surreal to re-embark on the regular routine of life after a major emotional ordeal. Colleagues laugh and carry on while I'm functioning in a daze. The attorney, Katie, who is my supervisor and close friend at this point, tells me she cannot believe I'm standing upright. "If I were you,

I would be sobbing uncontrollably with my head stuck in a bucket."

She gets a chuckle out of me. "Katie, that is maybe not one of the top ten helpful things to say."

Katie changes the subject. "By the way, Patricia barked at me today."

Patricia is a Child Protective Services worker. Her regular hairdo is reminiscent of Albert Einstein's, except it's black, not white. Based on my interactions with Patricia, I believe she's performing her job off her meds. Either that, or Patricia does not realize she needs meds.

Patricia is in the category of social workers from whom I would run away if they tried to take my children. We would be engaged in a tug-of-war. *You are not taking my kids. Sorry, send someone else. Preferably someone who doesn't present like a lunatic.*

I ask Katie to elaborate on the barking.

"I was standing outside the courtroom, waiting for our case to be called. Patricia walks up to me barking like a dog. I ask her what she's doing. She tells me I always bark orders at her, so she's barking back at me."

"Was it a Chihuahua dog bark, or, like, a St. Bernard dog bark? Rabid Labrador? I need details."

Katie turns to her desk photo of actor Denis Leary. There's a hand-drawn bubble next to his head that says, "I just love that Katie."

Katie says, "I cannot wait to get the fuck out of this crazy job. Denis Leary doesn't know I exist, but once he finds out, I'll be swept off my feet to the Hollywood Hills or a penthouse in Manhattan or wherever he lives. Could be Durham, North Carolina, for all I know. I don't care where it is as long as I'm out of this joint and together with Denis Leary, happily ever after."

Eventually, the office moves to a different location that does not include the built-in Muzak system that plays the hit song "ALL PARTIES . . ." all day, every day.

-6-

In April 2003 I give birth to Cynthia Rose. She's named after my late sister, Cindy. We call her Rose.

After maternity leave, I return to work. Every so often, I pull out my breast pump. Once, I pump while reviewing a medical record of a child who is diagnosed with failure to thrive—extreme low weight. The irony is strange.

I never intend to have more children. At home, I lie next to Rose on the bed and stare at her. She's perfect. I'm in bliss.

I plan a trip to Jamaica with two of my favorite humans on the planet, Charlie and Anita. Charlie and Anita are good friends of Ray's and mine. We met them when they lived in Richmond. They are smart and goofy and loads of fun to be around. Back when we first met, we spent a lot of time together.

I remember one of those times, back when Ray and I were married. Charlie, Anita, Ray, and I are sitting in our apartment. My daughter Melissa is spending the weekend with her aunt. We are all broke and bored.

Anita says, "Let's sneak into Busch Gardens. I used to work there. I know a way in."

We're all game.

We smoke a joint and arrive at the Germany parking lot at Busch Gardens, along with lots of other cars. The arrivals walk toward the tram that will transport them to the entrance. The four of us walk in the opposite direction, toward the woods.

Ray says, "Well, this isn't obvious at all."

Anita says, "Nobody's paying attention to us."

We trudge through the forest. Theme park music is playing in nearby Germany. It sounds like adventure music from an old cowboy flick—if it were set in Bavaria. We laugh in delight at having a soundtrack for our adventure.

Ray steps onto what looks like a large stand of moss—and discovers it's not moss, but a small pond covered in algae. Ray falls into the pond. He jumps out screaming and beats at the pond scum on his pants, yelling, "Leeches! Leeches!" Charlie, Anita, and I laugh.

We walk up to a gate. It's ajar. We slip into the park, trying to act nonchalant even though Ray is drenched in green slime.

Anita is right. Nobody pays attention to us.

❧

Now that Rose is born and I am no longer pregnant, I can start to think about that trip again. Wayne's parents are smitten with Rose, the granddaughter they never thought they would have. They are happy to have an extended visit with her while we vacation with Charlie and Anita in Jamaica.

Wayne and I exit the plane in Montego Bay. We pile into a rental car with Charlie, Anita, and their friendly buddy, Bill, and head to our rental house in Discovery Bay.

We arrive to beautiful doctor birds flying around the property, feeding on nectar from the blood-red hibiscus in the gardens. Set against the hibiscus, the birds' shimmering green feathers and long black tails make for a color scheme reminiscent of the traditional colors of the Rastas.

We listen to the sounds of parrots as we soak in the pool overlooking the turquoise bay. We sip daiquiris and Red Stripe beer on the porch, or perched in the hammock by the water. We have arrived in paradise.

I've never indulged in a vacation like it. And the luxury is surprisingly affordable—though I find out why when we venture out and see the poverty on the rest of the island.

Alfred is the friendly in-house chef. He appears beyond retirement age, but retirement is probably not an option for many of the working class in Jamaica. For a guy who cooks delicious food for a living, he's in good shape.

Alfred walks down to the dock and purchases fresh lobster from a boat. Then I join him in the kitchen. I have found an unsuspecting stranger to listen to my nonstop stories while I sip on a Red Stripe. I'm curious to know where he grew up, when he started cooking, whether he has siblings or a family, whether he likes living in Jamaica. Did he ever see Bob Marley?

Alfred is a quiet fellow. I have a feeling he would be perfectly content cooking supper without the distraction of an overly chatty tourist.

When supper is ready, we take a seat at the table on the porch overlooking the bay and feast on lobster, salad, rice, and corn fritters.

The next morning, breakfast is a smorgasbord of papaya, mango, pineapples, bananas, kiwi, ackee, and eggs. Our bellies are full and ready for a road trip to Nine Mile, the birthplace of Bob Marley, the artist who reigns supreme in my music world.

Bill is our driver, and he is very brave, as it quickly becomes apparent that driving in Jamaica is like playing Russian Roulette on a NASCAR track. I imagine a broadcaster: "The Maserati passes the Jaguar to take the lead! Did you see that tight pass at lightning speed around the sharp curve? Nearly wiped out the four-speed automatic Ford SUV traveling at thirty miles per hour with the five tourists! Folks, did you see the look on their faces?! Priceless!"

We stop at a roadside bar, which is not a bar in the traditional sense of the word, but more of an open-front shack. It's a lot like a burger stand; but all they sell is distilled spirits.

I get a drink, in the hope that it will reduce my back-seat screams of terror to mere fits of hushed panic: "I'll take a rum and Coke. Hold the Coke. Fill 'er to the rim."

We continue on to Nine Mile. I'm convinced the bright red soil along the road is soaked with the blood of travelers who have succumbed to NASCAR roulette.

Rows of cabbage and yam crops spread out in lines across the rolling hills, which are studded with shacks and topped with large concrete barrels that catch rainwater. The tiny, rundown shacks are a contradiction to the thriving plant life that surrounds them: ferns and palm trees edge the narrow, bumpy dirt road as it winds through the hills. In some places, it seems barely there—one wrong move, and a long drop down a steep embankment is an unfortunate possibility. Thank God for the intoxicating distraction of rum.

We arrive safely at Nine Mile, where I high-five Bill and

give him several hugs for his successful driving on the left side of the road.

Nine Mile is a small village tucked in a valley surrounded by high mountains. Bob Marley's mausoleum is the main attraction, and most likely the sole source of income for this poor, rundown village.

As we get out of the car, the smell of marijuana surrounds us. Men stand around and offer to sell us joints. We politely decline.

Charlie and Anita have traveled to Nine Mile several times before. They introduce us to Bob Marley's uncle, Lloyd.

Lloyd is a friendly fellow, a village elder with a Buddha-like smile that radiates goodness and happiness. Laughter comes easy to Lloyd.

He welcomes us with open arms to the row of square cinderblock shacks he and his extended family call home. Tin roofing and plywood serve as covers for the openings around the concrete frames. Inside, dirt floors and makeshift beds welcome us.

Clothes dry on lines hung around the homes, and more vegetable gardens surround the compound. Nine Mile is fertile—the soil is rich, the crops hearty.

Lloyd offers to feed us—a gracious gesture, considering the poverty of the village. Groups of children surround us and break into a song as happy as their beaming smiles. They want money, and we are happy to oblige. We hand out decks of cards, toothbrushes, and soap. I'm moved by the joyful spirit of the people of Nine Mile.

We visit Bob Marley's mausoleum. His song "Talkin' Blues" plays:

Cold ground was my bed last night
And rock was my pillow, too.

Wayne and I play dominoes at a bar owned by Bob Marley's sister, while Charlie leaves in search of his native islander friend, Benji. Benji comes to stay with us in Discovery Bay.

ↈ

We travel to Kingston to attend a birthday celebration for Bob Marley. High up in the Blue Mountains, we stop at a scenic pull-off boasting a view of a gorgeous mountain range with mile-high waterfalls. A group of Jamaicans approach and ask if we want to purchase Blue Mountain coffee beans.

Benji insists we purchase coffee from them. They will be upset with us if we purchase coffee from the café around the corner.

The group of Jamaican Coffee Entrepreneurs are on a mission. They lay out multiple ziplock baggies of coffee beans. I'm reminded of a seedy pot deal. I hold up the bags. I'm not a coffee bean connoisseur. They could be peddling Folgers, and I wouldn't know the difference.

"I'll take a pound." They eye me suspiciously. "Okay, two pounds. Can you cut me a deal on three pounds?"

We arrive in Kingston. I'm grateful for the presence of Benji. He knows how to navigate the city—a very important skill. We do not want to end up in Trench Town, where, we have been warned, one of the many gangs—much scarier than the Blue Mountain Coffee Gang—might surround our SUV and demand we exit the car if we want to live. Benji explains how stolen cars are sped away to illicit garages, where they are given a quick shiny new paint job and made ready to be resold on the black market.

We drive to Emancipation Park, the alleged scene of the birthday celebration. Except for a few families enjoying a day in the park with their kids, it's deserted.

Benji asks some folks around town about the celebration. He discovers there's a special event at the Bob Marley Museum on Hope Street.

We arrive at the museum and take a tour. The bullet holes from an assassination attempt on Bob Marley in 1976 are still visible, a peephole into the violence he condemned. We exit the museum to the birthday celebration, a welcome contrast to the unsettling image of the bullet holes inside the house.

Members of the Ethiopian Orthodox Church are playing Nyabinghi drums with elder Rastas. Nyabinghi music involves a lot of chanting and drumming—hymns of the Rastafarians to celebrate special occasions.

Charlie pokes me. "Check it out. Bunny Wailer is hanging out over there." Bunny Wailer is an original member of Bob Marley's band, the Wailers. Bunny Wailer gives a blessing when the birthday cake is pulled out. There's singing and chanting, incense burning, and reading of scriptures.

If there is a World Heritage Site of musical performances, Bob Marley's fifty-ninth birthday celebration is it. Elated energy surrounds us, amplified by the continual, spiritual sounds of Nyabinghi beats.

Several revelers are pointing at the moon and gasping. I turn around to see brilliant red, green, and gold bands surrounding the moon, shining through an unusual-looking cloud passing over the moon.

Bob Marley's son Ky-Mani Marley is on the stage. "I truly see a natural mystic tonight!"

The national newspaper, the *Jamaica Gleaner*, reports the event with the headline "Mystic Marley Moment": "Even the very heavens saluted Bob Marley on his 59th birthday. . . . The crowd roared and rocked as one, as the song crept in and then sang as one with Bob that there is a natural mystic blowing in the air."

We exit the Bob Marley celebration in awe. The party is still going strong. I'm energized by the night's event, which is a good thing: we have a long drive home ahead of us, and this time, I'm the designated driver, though I've never driven on the left side of the road.

We drive through the parish of Spanish Town in the wee hours of the morning. Groups of revelers gather on street corners and dance, accompanied by sound systems broadcasting "Stir It Up" and "Trench Town Rock." From the energy of the party, it seems Bob Marley's birthday is practically a national holiday.

The street celebrations continue through the night, in every parish we pass on the drive home. And so, our vacation in paradise comes to an end.

-7-

There was a time in my life when I was determined I would never remarry—a time when I thought my firstborn, Melissa, would be the sole child I would bear. I had big plans to join the Peace Corps when Melissa became an adult, and I committed to a maximum of five years at my sad job.

Now, on year number seven at my job, I have a one-year-old daughter—and I'm pregnant with my son. If the deals I made with myself are binding, I have good cause to pursue breach of contract.

But there's a dysfunctional allure to my job. I'm good at what I do, I'm committed to the cause—and I feel like less of a broken human when I read the cases. It's *like* being in the Peace Corps—but I get to stay home instead of being sent to Africa to eradicate malaria and maybe get eaten by a hippo.

To say my third pregnancy was emotionally difficult is like saying Donald Trump is a wee bit moody.

My marriage somehow survives the fits and starts of my wild mood swings, which feel like a ride on the Loch Ness roller coaster at Busch Gardens—the hundred-foot drop, up and around the intertwining loops, and through a dark tunnel, coasting toward a finish line that seems like it will never come. I'm so hormonal that when George W. Bush is reelected, I march past the break room at work in a rage and proclaim, "I'M MOVING TO CANADA."

The attorneys and staff are gathered in the break room, eating lunch. If they want to laugh, they don't. They all know how tense I've been during the last few months.

After I calm down, I join the crew in the break room. Wayne comes to visit with Rose so that I can nurse her. On the way, he stops to say hello to Elana, a friend of mine who works in the office as an administrative assistant. Wayne plays bass in her band, a group of talented rock-and-roll musicians.

A funny, beautiful woman from Queens who is as honest and soulful in conversation as she is in song, Elana adds wonderful spice to the office. One day, she came flying by my desk in a panic. She ran out the back door, around the building, and back through the front door, circling several times and moaning, "Oh my God, oh my God . . ."

"What's the matter, honey?" I ask as she flies by me.

"My ear is ringing. What if I'm losing my hearing? Oh my God, oh my God . . ."

"Honey, it's okay," I try to reassure her.

"This is very bad. I may never sing again. Oh my God. Hold on. Wait. Okay—it stopped. I can hear again. What if this is temporary, and the ringing returns?" Elana is pacing in circles. Music means everything to her.

But the ringing does not return—much to everyone's relief.

Now, Elana answers the main work phone next to the break room where I'm nursing Rose and hanging out with a few of the attorneys. Our coworker Cerelia has gone home due to stomach pain, and now she calls Elana, wailing in agony. She needs to go to the bathroom, but nothing is moving.

Elana, bless her heart, is not first on the list of calm individuals to speak to about anything related to medical conditions. She says, "Hold on, honey; I'm going to see if I can figure out what's going on with you. Hold on, okay?"

Elana appears in the break room in a panic. "Is there such a thing as an anal aneurysm?"

I bust out laughing so hard, I have to hand Rose over to Wayne. I can barely speak through the uncontrollable laughter that consumes me.

"I'm sorry—it's just—anal aneurysm—it's not funny, I know—I'm sorry." I wipe away tears. I have no control over the fit of laughter that overcomes me.

Years later, my boss, Katie, would reflect on my pregnancy: "There were times I worried that your head was going to start spinning around and pea soup would spew out of your mouth."

I pray—and my prayers are not the prayers of my past, when I pleaded that my loved ones would be safe and healthy. Instead I pray to God, Jah, Buddha, Venus, the Moon, and the Sun that I'll survive these mood swings. Compared to this one, my other pregnancies were a day in the park.

I sit at my desk, trying to remain upright. I'm overcome with deep depression. Everything seems so overwhelmingly sad—the reelection of President Bush, the war in Iraq, rampant child abuse—it's all too much.

I walk out of the office and into an alley that leads to the parking deck. The soft fluttering of my son moving inside my belly is the most enthusiastic part of my being.

An old man dressed in baggy pants, a bulky canvas Army coat, and a raggedy knit hat is sorting through trash in a dumpster in the alley. He looks worse for wear, as though he has spent his entire life digging through dumpsters.

The old man looks up as I walk by him. His face lights up, his smile so big and kind it grabs my attention. He says, "It's okay, honey; everything is going to be alright."

This homeless man offering kind words to me causes me to pause and consider my many blessings. I still get chills when I think about that man.

༄

I call Mom to check in. Mom says, "Did you hear George Bush was reelected? Did you know he used to be director of the CIA? He must be a decent man. Barbara Bush is just wonderful."

"Mom, his son was reelected. You're a Democrat. What part of being the head of the CIA do you correlate with being decent?"

Mom struggles with day-to-day responsibilities: paying bills, cooking, keeping house. Robert lives with her. He drives her around town and keeps her company, but that's the extent of the assistance he offers.

Mom asks me how I am doing. I say, "You should see my belly. This is one big baby."

Mom says, "You're pregnant? Oh, that's wonderful."

I break the news that I'm pregnant every time we talk.

ↄ

Charles is born two years to the day after his sister Rose was born. He's named after my father. He's a strapping baby with an appetite to match. My mood swings calm down after his birth. It's a good thing. Tending to a newborn is serious business—especially when that newborn insists on nursing so frequently, my milk often runs dry.

When I return to my job after the birth, I work for four attorneys. I receive at least one case a day, and sometimes two, or even five. The court schedules the initial hearings within three days. I order medical records and school records. I must provide them to the opposing counsel twenty-four hours prior to the hearing. I subpoena and interview police officers and medical experts. Every few hours, I pull out my electric breast pump while I work on cases involving babies born addicted to cocaine and opiates, or a toddler that someone used as a punching bag.

The job goes from manageable to out-of-control busy within minutes. I beg Katie to hire help for me.

My plea for help comes through, and a part-time paralegal is hired. Mark is a fifty-something-year-old choral director. His John Lennon-style eyeglasses add an air of charm to his otherwise crotchety disposition. Every so often, a cheery character emerges, like the miracle of the sun peeking through heavy cloud cover.

Mark is socially awkward. He compensates for his oddball demeanor by being haughty to everyone in the office—except the beautiful pregnant attorney he has a crush on.

Mark is married to the pastor of the church where he is a choir director. One day, she comes into the office to meet

Mark for lunch. She is beautiful, with long, thick dark hair and a disposition that makes me think she could cure world hunger. If there is a pastoral air for a pastor, she exemplifies it.

After Mark returns from lunch, he asks me whether I'm wondering how he managed to score a wife like her. Mark lets on that he had a difficult childhood. He doesn't fully elaborate, but he mentions spending time in an orphanage. He says it makes the work we do challenging for him.

I assign casework to Mark. "Please order medical records. We need them by tomorrow."

I have worked very hard to form positive relationships with the medical record departments, as I routinely request they drop everything and help me out on a day's notice. I cringe when I hear Mark yelling on the telephone. "If you don't get the records to me by tomorrow, I'll subpoena your supervisor to court!"

It's not starting off well.

Mark sends Sarah, the beautiful pregnant attorney an email—not asking if he can get her something from the cafe across the street. Not a question about a case he's working on. Mark reworks Edgar Allan Poe's "The Raven" into a poem about the impending birth. There are many references to the baby rapping and tapping on her chamber door.

Sarah forwards the email to the office. We all agree it's a head-scratcher.

Another email to Sarah advises her that the air in her left rear tire is a little low. She better have her husband go fill it with air as soon as possible.

Mark continues sabotaging professional connections I

work hard to maintain. Social workers do not like his rude attitude. I start giving him work that does not involve communicating with anyone. I'd rather go it alone than deal with Mark.

As if to confirm the shittiness of my job, the receptionist hands me an envelope that contains paperwork for a new case. I open up the envelope and look at the photos attached to the case. My heart falls into my abdomen.

One case out of every couple hundred strikes close to the hearts of the attorneys who get it. It's the gold medal of horrible cases. For me, this is the Triple Crown of those gold-medal cases. I'm devastated. How can a human be capable of such evil?

I tell my boss Katie to refer me to the free therapy that is available to city employees.

When my appointment arrives, I sit down with the therapist I've been assigned and tell him about the case—but I may have been in his office for ten minutes before he waves his hand and says, "Oh, I think you're handling it fine."

"Actually, no, I'm not. I wouldn't be here if I was handling it fine."

"I'm not going to recommend you receive further therapy. I honestly don't think you need it."

I conclude that the therapist could not handle the facts of the case. It's another therapy fail. At least I have a supportive husband and the delight of Rose and Charles to look forward to at the end of the day.

When Charles is around a year old, Wayne and I move into his parents' home. They need to scale down to a smaller house, and we need to scale up and away from the house next door to us, which has been turned into a halfway house for recovering crack and heroin addicts. I do not want my children to live their lives locked inside, with their parents staring out the windows in guarded fear.

✑

Mom's dementia progresses to the point that she needs to move to an assisted living facility. A few weeks after I complete the arduous task of moving my own immediate family, my sisters and I gather at her home to sort through and pack up the belongings that Mom has accumulated over the past forty years.

I say, "Mom saved my report cards. I could have contended for the Dishonorable Society. This one says I speak out of turn and I don't pay attention."

We look through the numerous photo albums Mom put together. The 1982 album has photos of me from my junior year of high school. "That was when anorexia was in fashion. God, I look horrible."

With Mom in her new home at the assisted living facility, our brother Robert has to move, too. Robert now weighs over three hundred pounds, and he has horrible allergies and sleep apnea. We look for a place for him to live, and find a small apartment in a subsidized housing complex in the heart of Williamsburg. The move away from the home where he has lived for forty-odd years must be a huge adjustment. He visits Mom every day, and stays with her for hours.

My parents were Robert's life. His only close companions. I'm worried about him.

I visit Robert periodically to check on him. When I knock, he won't let me inside. He cracks open the door, and through the sliver of an opening, I can see piles of clothes and old food containers littering the small apartment.

I ask Robert if he is using his sleep apnea machine. He responds in anger. "Don't worry about it."

Robert's face is puffy. His bloodshot eyes disappear behind bulging skin. He shuts the door and tells me to go away. He is not the gentle, sweet soul I knew and adored.

The sight of Robert causes an uncontrollable eruption of tears. I call my sister Sara with a desperate plea that we must do something to help Robert, but I can barely speak. When I try to calm down, my body doesn't cooperate.

A week later, my sister Kris calls me at work with the news that Robert has died in his sleep.

At Robert's service, Mom sits in the front row, wearing a black suit, stockings, and pumps. Her arms are folded atop her crossed legs. She's a vision of grace.

I'm not sure if she comprehends that her son is dead.

Mom's expression is bare of emotion, but her blue eyes sparkle. I wonder if it's the shimmer of unshed tears, or the shine of blissful ignorance.

I will never forget my last, heartbreaking sight of Robert. My sweet brother. Even the school bullies had been nice to Robert. He had played the tuba in the band. He had a kind smile, and he was always happy. Everyone liked Robert.

Back in my cubicle at work, I review a psychological evaluation of an adolescent who has been diagnosed with bipolar disorder, ADHD, and depression. She came to the attention of social services after six suicide attempts. Her single mother cannot handle her behavior.

Katie flies into my office. "Come with me." When I ask her why, she says, "I can't give you any details. Come on."

Katie, Mark, and I pile into Katie's car. Mark is pleading from the back seat. "Just because I said I feel like checking out does not mean I want to kill myself. I'm fine, boss. Come on; let's go back to the office."

What the hell is going on? I wonder.

We arrive at Tucker's Psychiatric Hospital. The waiting room is a spectacle of everything one would expect at a psychiatric facility: a bunch of visibly crazy people. I think, *I don't get paid enough for this.* Mark looks pissed off.

Katie whispers to me, "Don't look now, but there's a four-hundred-pound guy sitting to your left that has elephantiasis testicles."

Katie's delivery is deadpan and unexpected. I bust out laughing. Mark is on the other side of me, seething. If there was ever a "Calgon, take me away!" moment, this is it.

Katie fills me in on the situation that caused the emergency trip to the hospital. It turns out Katie is on a mission to save Mark. Mark confesses he was caught kissing women at his church. He's depressed, and says he sometimes feels like checking out.

After the hospital incident, Mark continues to send Sarah emails on a regular basis. Some of the emails mention how nice she looks. Others are just strange. One of the emails indicates that he's following up on a case regarding Peter Piper. Turns out Peter Piper picked less than the contractually agreed-upon peck of pickled peppers.

One afternoon, I walk over to Mark's cubicle to give him a file. I'm wearing a black knit dress, blue tights, and leather boots. Mark looks me up and down, and says, "What made you think that's a good outfit?"

I laugh. Then I am nearly knocked over by the smell of whiskey on his breath.

It's one more issue to add to the dysfunction at the office. My workday reality is full of abused children and a creepy coworker who sends inappropriate emails and drinks on the job.

I sit down with the receptionist, Linda, and tell her about Mark's drinking. Linda is a sweet and jolly woman. We often sit in her office and share the latest news of what's happening in our lives.

When I tell her about Mark, Linda says, "Really? Maybe he's drinking because of his back pain. Or this job." Despite Mark's rude demeanor, Linda never says an ill word about him. Now, she moves on. "Last night, my husband says, 'Linda, come here. Look at this.' I go to the den, and there's a big ol' slimy whale on the TV. I say, 'What makes you think I'm interested in a damn whale?'"

Linda has a serious issue with her husband's love of the Discovery Channel. As she tells me this story, she looks as though she just ate something foul.

I say, "You know, people pay money to watch whales. They're fascinating creatures."

Linda says, "You couldn't pay me to go watch a damn whale!"

❦

I'm sitting in my boss, Katie's, office, catching up. Katie is holding a plastic Martian stress doll. It's one of the gifts I gave her for Christmas. When she first opened the gift she said, "What the hell is this?" She was not impressed. Now, she uses the Martian regularly.

Katie is squeezing the doll as we talk. Its ears, eyes, and nose pop in and out with every squeeze. Katie asks in her typical deadpan tone, "How many cases have we gotten? Any dead babies?" Squeeze. Pop! I burst out laughing and think, *This is one for the book.*

I say, "No, but I'm working on a case regarding twelve children, all of whom have names that begin with Qu followed by different sequences of vowels with a few random consonants thrown in. The only difference in two of the names is one has 'ae' in the middle and the other one has 'ea'. Mother is a prostitute and a crack addict."

Katie throws a pen across the room and yells, "I fucking hate people."

Later, Katie asks me, "How are the kids? Tell me you're not still serving on that stupid board of directors at the fairy school."

Rose and Charles attend a Waldorf school, which offers a creative approach to learning. They have a class called eurythmy, where the kids don colorful silk capes and dance around in a circle in expressive movements of joy and sorrow. Charles doesn't like it. He expresses his sorrow by sitting out, pouting, and calling eurythmy stupid.

Katie laughs. "Oh my God, do you remember the time

you were so bored at the board meeting that you stood up and said, 'My family needs me!' and ran out?"

ᗑ

I walk back to my cubicle. Mark is stumbling around the office. He's half lit.

He's not a cheery drunk.

ᗑ

My telephone rings. It's the manager of the assisted living facility where Mom resides. She says there's been an incident. Another resident barricaded my Mom in her room with him and raped her.

My heart falls. I demand to know how such a thing could happen. What kind of security do they have? The manager says, "Maybe your mother liked it."

I'm devastated. *My mother has been raped, and you're suggesting she may have* liked *it?!* Good lord.

I want to reach through the telephone and knock her out.

I immediately bolt to my car and drive to see Mom. When I get there, I embrace her. She pushes me away. She's agitated, nonverbal. She paces around the room, motioning from the door to the bed with her arms. Mom waves her arms in circles over the bed like it's the scene of the crime. I fight back tears.

My sisters and I immediately find another assisted living facility, and move Mom.

-8-

It's July 17, 2014—year number fifteen at my job. I wonder why I haven't run away screaming. I have no good reason, other than the fact that I am a crazy person.

I receive a call from the new facility where Mom lives. Her time has come.

Mom is now eighty-five years old. Even though her body and mind have disintegrated, she always has a sweet expression on her face.

I'm bedside with Mom. The nurses are very upset about her imminent passing. "She's our sweet, sweet Phyllis," they say.

I sit still. *I'm going to be with Mom when she takes her last breath, just like she was with me when I took my first breath.*

I rub Mom's forehead, and her thick mane of white hair.

I remember all the times I sat at the kitchen table while Mom cooked or ironed or sat with me chatting. In one of these memories, Mom and I are watching birds in the backyard. I'm fourteen years old. It's winter. The forest beyond the yard stretches beyond our view.

I say, "Mom, the bare trees depress me."

Mom, who grew up in Duluth, Minnesota and has an affinity for winter, says, "They are baring their souls to us. I think they're beautiful."

From that moment on, I love bare trees.

I remember lying on the bed with Mom. In this memory,

she puts her book down, and I ask her what she is reading. It's a book about the discovery of ancestors and their stories. She says, "Did you know your great-great-grandfather's name was Chris Kringel? He immigrated from Denmark in 1870 at age two. When his father lived in Denmark, they changed the surname system because there were too many Andersons and Christensons. His father picked Kringel, because they lived on Kringel Creek."

I remember another moment. This time, I'm nineteen years old. Mom and I sit on the front porch in the webbed green aluminum rocking chairs. Mom says, "Have you ever done psychedelic mushrooms?"

I say, "Why do you ask?"

Mom says, "The book I'm reading mentions they can be a tool for spiritual healing."

I say, "Mom, promise me you will not take mushrooms. Seriously. You are not a good candidate. I cannot handle the thought of you on mushrooms."

Mom says, "Don't you worry," and chuckles.

I pick up the book Mom put together for all of us kids one Christmas. It's titled *Readings, Writings, Recipes, and Repertoire,* and includes the piano music she composed and dedicated to each of us, as well as some of her favorite recipes. (Exhibit A of the food I consumed on a daily basis growing up: Watergate Pudding—crushed pineapple, a large container of Cool Whip, a package of pistachio pudding, chopped nuts, and miniature marshmallows.)

It also includes the assignments Mom wrote when she took a creative writing class when I was in high school.

For one piece, Mom interviewed our neighbor, Hanni.

Hanni's father had been an editor in Germany. He was the first to warn people about Hitler. One day, Hanni, her siblings, and their mother went to visit Hanni's grandmother. On the way home, a family friend intercepted them. He told them they could not return home. Their father had been killed. The friend had an understanding with the border guards in Switzerland. Hanni and her siblings hid in the trunk. The friend told the border guards he was taking a lady friend out drinking, and they escaped to Switzerland.

Life in Switzerland, however, was horrible. So Hanni made her way to America, where she went to college, and eventually became a German language teacher at the high school I attended.

I read another piece my Mom wrote:

Here's to Me: Central High School, Class of '47
Here's to me. Us. All of us: Sleeping beauties,
Cinderellas.
Dreamers.
We were conceived in the garden of plenty, but borne
into the vale of depression. Seeing our parents' fears, we
tried to iron away their anxieties with laughter and
eagerness to please. We were poor but knew it not. We
never heard of breadlines or dust bowls.
Taught by spinsters whose lives were committed to us,
we collected stamps, went bird-watching, twirled batons,
played the cello, learned to draw free-hand and make our
letters as perfect as Mary Louise Shopbell. We never heard
of Nazis, Fascists and Totalitarianism.
We entered puberty to the march of savings stamps,

war bonds, Kamikaze, buzz bonds, concentration camps and air raid warnings. We had nightmares.

But—we wore sloppy joe sweaters, pleated skirts, bobby socks and saddle shoes. We wore our hair in page boys. If we wanted to be sophisticated we painted our legs. We wrote volumes of letters, wrote in our diaries, went to the prom by transit bus, skated, skied, planted victory gardens, played the clarinet, tried cigarettes, went to church every Sunday, prayed for peace. We never heard of homosexuals, Freud, birth control, hydrogen bombs, and rockets to the moon or equal rights.

We dreamed. Of fame, of marriage, of Prince Charming, of success. Some of us grew up to be Beverly Sills, Jacqueline Kennedy Onassis, Princess Grace, Shirley Temple. Most of us grew up to be teachers, nurses, secretaries and housewives.

Our dreams come true.

Now all the things we never heard of begin to haunt us. Now we want to know, we want to learn, we want to think. We want to face the anxieties—not iron them away or laugh them into non-existence.

Here's to me.

Here's to us.

I read this piece, too:

There was a time that I liked it—rock music. (I was teaching it to teen-agers. To teach it one needs to understand it. Understanding helps liking it.) But not now. I don't dislike it; I'm just neutral. Kathy likes it: she LOVES it. She loves it as I love opera. To Kathy, rock is her music;

opera is mine. Sometimes rock and opera have nothing in common because we have nothing in common. Other times, when Kathy and I are in tune with each other, we understand each other's needs to want desperately to sing our own music.

But I don't want to hear Kathy using that raucous, cheerleading, breathless tone quality any more than she likes my round, full-voiced, dramatic vibrato. But she loves the sensuous continuing rock rhythm: the fast, exciting pulse that doesn't allow for repose. That unceasing movement is even there in "mellow rock." "When does all this end?" I cry. "I expect that someday I'll see it still undulating along searching for heaven's gate."

"How can you like opera?" and off she goes to play her records—LOUD—in her own room.

Opera. My music comes to me through my little radio above the sink. Soft and intimate. It is expressive, beautiful, singing. In opera everything hangs out: love, despair, hate, glory. Peter Grimes' agony, Mimi's sweet helplessness, the ecstasy of Octavian and Sophie, Wotan's anger. I've seen opera—once or twice—with its glory and pageantry. But I like it in my kitchen so I can cry a little or sing along—loud—if the spirit moves me.

I wonder whether rock—with its restless spirit and opera with its ponderous verbosity, I wonder whether they speak to a level of growth in us, or whether they are more part of our personality that needs that kind of expression. Kathy and I will probably never come to terms with each other's passions. Perhaps we can understand that the music we love fulfills our own needs to express ourselves.

I never told Mom that I eventually grew to appreciate opera. I've actually attended a few live performances. But I appreciate her honesty.

❧

I look at Mom, there in her bed, and I desire to be the selfless and even-tempered human she is. I'm grateful that I inherited her love for the written word, her capacity to forgive. Her commitment. I deeply regret how much of a pain in the ass I was.

My sister Kris and her twenty-some-year-old daughter Nikki walk into the room. I have no idea how long we will be here before Mom passes. I do know that if this had happened two days later, my family would be in upstate New York. I may not have been able to be with Mom.

Perhaps she somehow knew. Perhaps she did not want to burden anyone by dying at an inconvenient time. That would be just like her.

Kris and Nikki settle into chairs next to Mom's bed. Nikki recalls the time that Mom invited her, my nephew, and my daughter Melissa over for a weekend, completely out of the blue. The kids were around ten and twelve years old at the time. It was midnight, and they were up giggling and being loud. Mom, who was always early to bed, got so mad. No one ever saw Mom angry. She came into the bedroom, shaking her finger. "You get to bed right now!"

Nikki laughs. She says, "We had to cover our mouths because we were laughing that Grandma was mad."

Kris and I laugh. I look over to Mom—and she's gone. Just like that. Maybe the laughter was comforting for her.

The nurses weep when she passes away. "She was our sweet, sweet Phyllis."

The managing nurse comes into the room and asks us how we would like to dispose of the body. I find her question cold. *This is my kind, talented, wonderful mother you are talking about. How do I want to dispose of her? What are my options? I want the best disposal option.*

I call a funeral home. Then Kris, Nikki, and I sit in the room with Mom's body for about an hour, before I go out to pace in the hallway.

The undertaker arrives. He says, "I've come to dispose of your loved one."

What's with the cold demeanor of these people? My mother just passed away. Could you be a little gentler? But I guess if your job is disposing of dead bodies, you probably aren't a Mr. Rogers kind of guy.

Two days after Mom's passing, Wayne and I travel to the Hudson Valley to drop our kids off at summer camp. Then we spend the week with my sister Sara and her husband Dana in New Jersey, planning Mom's funeral.

Mom made it clear she wanted to be cremated. Sara is on the telephone with the funeral home. She says, "Twenty-five hundred bucks for an urn? Do you have anything cheaper?"

After she hangs up, Dana says, "Man, I can get an urn for ninety-nine bucks on eBay."

Sara says, "Dana!"

What follows is some of the darkest humor I've ever participated in—ever.

Dana says, "Look, here's a lava lamp on eBay. It's sixteen ninety-nine. We can put her in there and place her on the mantle. Every once in a while, we'll say, 'Look! There she is.'"

Sara and I are crying, we are laughing so hard—an uncontrollable fit of wine-induced hysterics. When I settle down, I say, "Take it back. Mom doesn't deserve to have her remains placed in a lava lamp. However, we may be on to something here. Let's start advertising lava lamp urns on eBay. The ad will say, 'Do you hate your loved one? When you think of them, does the word "evil" come to mind? The Lava Lamp Urn may be for you!'"

One of Mom's former piano students, Karen, reaches out to me to tell me that my mother changed her life. Karen tells me she loved Mom so much.

I loved Mom, too. I wrote this piece about my parents. It's called "Always."

Today I read a piece by NPR Weekend Edition host Scott Simon titled, "We Don't Fully Grow Up Until We Lose Our Parents." I had the sudden realization that my parents are gone. It comes to me like that. Every once in a while, I have an "aha" moment. Oh right, my parents are gone. I lost both of my parents to Alzheimer's disease. I lost them slowly for at least ten years before their bodies left this planet.

When I think of them, it's typically Mom ironing my father's shirts, the scent of spray starch, the Metropolitan Opera playing on a cheap radio and Mom singing along in her alto voice. The sound of a college football game in the background. Dad is fishing on the beach in the Outer Banks, or dressed up and looking sharp in his "monkey suit," as he called his tuxedo, before heading out to direct a concert band performance.

The last few times I saw my parents when they were alive was when they were non-verbal, wheelchair-bound and being fed by a nurse. But that is never how I remember them. Not through defiance or any conscious choice. It just isn't my "default memory." It's a strange thing, the body and the mind. I sat by Mom's side when she died last July. Her beautiful shell with her beautiful blue eyes that sparkled with a kindness that never waned no matter how far gone her mind was.

The nurses wept when she passed away. "She was our sweet, sweet Phyllis." I, being attracted to minds more than appearances, thought to myself, I lost her eight or ten years ago. There is no actual point of loss. It occurs to me every once in a while that my parents' bodies are gone, but I don't know when I really lost them. They're gone but they're not gone. They are singing opera and fishing, just like they always have.

-9-

Rose is four years old, and she is suffering from severe eczema. It's embarrassing, and the constant itching is miserable. Meanwhile, I'm contending with my own chronic anxiety, depression, and generally feeling like I missed out on the genetic lottery. The default feeling of my life.

I discover a study from the Henry Ford Department of Health Sciences: "C-section Babies Five Times More Likely to Develop Allergies"—the reason being that birth via a mother's birth canal exposes a newborn to healthy bacteria, whereas C-section babies are instead exposed to more unhealthy bacteria from the air. All of my children were born via C-section.

Next, I read an article about the human microbiome—the trillions of bacteria, viruses, and fungi that inhabit our bodies. Groundbreaking research has connected the health of the microbiome to multiple diseases, including mental health disorders, Parkinson's disease, Alzheimer's disease, obesity, and food allergies.

For this article, a group of microbiologists are asked what they believe plays a role in shaping the human microbiome. The top four answers are the method of birth, length of breastfeeding, early exposure to antibiotics, and lifetime exposure to antibiotics.

Mom did not breastfeed me, and I was on loads of antibiotics as a child and young adult. I'm fairly certain my microbiome is royally screwed up.

Reading that study sends me down a rabbit hole of medical research. I search for clinical trials about the correlation between food allergies and mental health issues. For the first time in my life, I am optimistic that a solution may be on the horizon. As I read, a bigger picture begins to emerge.

I learn from a study by cardiologist William Davis that the peptides in gliadin—an enzyme found in wheat—mimic an opiate in the brain. The same way a drug addict needs another hit, wheat stimulates an insatiable appetite for junk carbohydrates. Cheese produces a similar opiate effect—which is why it's so addictive. What's more, allergies to food can also upset levels of hormones and other key chemicals in the brain, resulting in symptoms ranging from depression and anxiety to schizophrenia.

I read a book called *Why Isn't My Brain Working?* by Dr. Datis Kharrazian, a specialist in the field of chronic, neurological, and autoimmune disorders. He elaborates on a study he coauthored with world-renowned immunologist Aristo Vojidani, which found that ". . . a significant portion of the US population not only reacts to gluten and dairy but also that this reaction causes the immune system to destroy brain and nervous tissue in a scenario called neurological autoimmunity (as evidenced by positive tissue antibodies). With the explosion of Alzheimer's, Parkinson's, autism, childhood development disorders, and other brain disorders happening today, these findings confirm what many clinicians have already seen in their practice: removing gluten and dairy from the diet has a profoundly positive impact on brain health in many people."

I read in a study published by the *Lancet* medical journal, titled "Nutritional Medicine as Mainstream in Psychiatry," about how "[p]sychiatry is at an important juncture, with the current pharmacologically focused model having achieved modest benefits in addressing the burden of poor mental health worldwide. Although the determinants of mental health are complex, the emerging and compelling evidence for nutrition as a crucial factor in the high prevalence and incidence of mental disorders suggests that diet is as important to psychiatry as it is to cardiology, endocrinology, and gastroenterology. Evidence is steadily growing for the relation between dietary quality (and potential nutritional deficiencies) and mental health, and for the select use of nutrient-based supplements to address deficiencies, or as monotherapies or augmentation therapies."

I read about how some recent studies have shown that as many as a third of depression sufferers may not respond to antidepressants at all. In light of this, the psychiatric community has begun to explore nutritional approaches to treating mental health disorders. But for too many people, it may be too late. One study on "Glucose Levels and Risk of Dementia," published in the *New England Journal of Medicine*, shows that even in people without diabetes, above-average blood sugar is associated with an increased risk of developing dementia. This finding goes beyond previously observed links between diabetes and dementia: "It establishes for the first time, convincingly, that there is a link between dementia and elevated blood sugars in the non-diabetic range, says study author Dr. David Nathan, a Harvard Medical School professor and the director of the Diabetes Center and Clinical Research Center at Massachusetts General Hospital."

I read, and make notes, and I begin to wonder if my own mental health issues, and my parents' dementia might be related—at least in part—to the high sugar and junk food diets we subsisted on for most of our lives.

I radically clean up my and my family's diet. I remove gluten, dairy, and sugar. It's a big deal for me, because I may be one of the top ten cheese-lovers on the planet.

Rose's eczema clears up. The chronic sinus issues that have thrown me to my knees throughout my life disappear. My haze of depression and anxiety lifts. My mood stabilizes. I feel dramatically better—both mentally and physically. For the first time in my life, I'm comfortable in my skin.

(By the way, if you go to a party and mention how great you feel now that you are gluten and dairy free, people will walk away and find someone else to talk to.)

As part of my ongoing crusade to overhaul my family's health, I also start taking magnesium supplements. A study published in 2017, titled "Role of Magnesium Supplementation in the Treatment of Depression: A Randomized Clinical Trial," tested 126 adults with mild to moderate depression. Participants were given 248 mg of magnesium a day for six weeks. Effects were observed within two weeks. The trial concluded that magnesium is effective for mild to moderate depression in adults without the need for close monitoring for toxicity.

I'm prepared to believe it. I've tried medication for my anxiety and depression. Nothing helped, and I got a big helping of unpleasant side effects. But the magnesium has a profound effect on my inner world and addictive tendencies.

One night, my husband and I return home from an evening out. I walk into the master bathroom and see water spilling out of the tub and flooding the floor. As I calmly turn off the water, my daughter walks in and says, "Oh my God, Mom! I totally forgot about the bath!"

Historically, this would have been a high-volume situation—with the volume mostly coming from me. Instead, I say, "It's okay, honey; accidents happen. Don't worry about it." My ability to handle stress has leveled out beyond anything I could have thought possible.

❧

Unfortunately, healthy food and vitamins are not affordable or attainable for everyone. I think back on some of the cases I've worked at my job over the past nineteen years. The most common picture of a family involved in the child welfare system consists of families of color, often living in public housing that is racially segregated in all but name. Parents are typically undereducated and contend with un- or underdiagnosed mental health disorders, which often results in substance abuse in the absence of affordable medical treatment. Many parents are themselves victims of childhood abuse.

I've reviewed hundreds of psychological evaluations of

parents and adolescents in the child welfare system, and followed their cases and their progress. They are typically on a lot of medications, and engaged in services to treat substance abuse and mental health. Despite this, positive outcomes are rare. From what I've seen, the current protocol of treating opioid addiction is rarely successful—and the drug epidemic is at an all-time high. There was a time when opiate use on its own was enough to warrant automatic removal of children from the home. Now it doesn't.

But even if it did, Richmond's Department of Housing and Urban Development is one of the most troubled HUD agencies in the country, with conditions in many of its facilities practically unlivable. As a result, I've always felt that the involvement of child welfare services in these communities is, at the end of the day, more punitive than restorative. After all, a charge of child abuse or neglect makes it difficult for a parent to obtain a job. I believe much of what I have observed in my job is symptomatic of ongoing socio-economic issues that have gone unaddresed for far too long.

☙

Thomas comes to visit me. In fact, he visits often. His is one of the few opiate addiction success stories I've ever seen. He has been clean for years.

Unfortunately, Thomas suffers from myotonic dystrophy, a condition similar to muscular dystrophy. His father and brother also had the condition. He uses a cane with a duck-head handle to get around.

I read him a headline from *The Onion*.

"The headline says, 'Iowa Fashion Week Begins.' This is the cutting edge of Iowa style. There's a photo of a woman dressed in jeans, a solid green T-shirt, and a plain coat."

Thomas laughs. "That's great." Then he says, "Did you know Iowa is the number one producer of corn, soy, pork, and eggs?"

"Yes."

"Really?"

"No."

Thomas proclaims his love for me. I return the sentiment. We go out to the deck, where he brings up a news story about whatever nonsense Donald Trump has been up to lately. I say, "That guy is wacky on the junk." Thomas laughs.

Then he says, "Did you know Robert E. Lee was against the Civil War?"

Bibliography

These references are not intended as a substitute for professional medical advice, diagnosis, or treatment, and do not constitute medical or other professional advice.

Kharrazian, Datis. *Why Isn't My Brain Working? A Revolutionary Understanding of Brain Decline and Effective Strategies to Recover Your Brain's Health.* Carlsbad, CA: Elephant Press, 2013.

Jerome Sarris, PhD, et al, "Nutritional Medicine as Mainstream in Psychiatry," *The Lancet Psychiatry*, Jan. 25, 2015.

Paul K. Crane MD, et al, "Glucose Levels and Risk of Dementia," *The New England Journal of Medicine*, Aug. 8, 2013.

Emily K. Tarelton, Benjamin Littenberg. "Role of Magnesium Supplementation in the Treatment of Depression: A Randomized Clinical Trial," *PLOS One*, June 27, 2017.

About the Author

Kathy Varner lives in Richmond, Virginia. She's a paralegal by trade, but a writer by passion. When she's not working or writing, you may find her gardening, cooking, hiking with her Shelties, dancing to her husband's bands, reading, and laughing. One day, she hopes that you will find her riding her bike through the Outer Hebrides in Scotland.

CPSIA information can be obtained
at www.ICGtesting.com
Printed in the USA
LVHW030905240120
644650LV00001B/1

9 781951 565138